Early Theories of Translation

Flora Ross Amos

ISBN: 9798526411899

Cover: *Saint Jerome in His Study*, by Vincenzo di Biagio Catena.

Submitted in Partial Fulfilment of the Requirements for the Degree of Doctor of Philosophy, in the Faculty of Philosophy, Columbia University.

Original publication: Columbia University Press, 1920

To my father and my mother

Table of Contents

PREFACE..7

I. The Medieval Period...13

II. The Translation of the Bible..................................57

III. The Sixteenth Century...87

IV. From Cowley to Pope..135

PREFACE

In the following pages I have attempted to trace certain developments in the theory of translation as it has been formulated by English writers. I have confined myself, of necessity, to such opinions as have been put into words, and avoided making use of deductions from practice other than a few obvious and generally accepted conclusions. The procedure involves, of course, the omission of some important elements in the history of the theory of translation, in that it ignores the discrepancies between precept and practice, and the influence which practice has exerted upon theory; on the other hand, however, it confines a subject, otherwise impossibly large, within measurable limits. The chief emphasis has been laid upon the sixteenth century, the period of the most enthusiastic experimentation, when, though it was still possible for the translator to rest in the comfortable medieval conception of his art, the New Learning was offering new problems and new ideals to every man who shared in the intellectual awakening of his time. In the matter of theory, however, the age was one of beginnings, of suggestions, rather than of finished, definitive results; even by the end of the century there were still translators who had not yet appreciated the immense difference between medieval and modern standards of translation. To understand their position, then, it is necessary to consider both the preceding period, with its incidental, half-unconscious comment, and the seventeenth and eighteenth centuries, with their systematized, unified contribution. This last material, in especial, is included chiefly because of the light which it throws in retrospect on the views of earlier translators, and only the main course of theory, by this time fairly easy to follow, is traced.

The aim has in no case been to give bibliographical information. A number of translations, important in themselves, have received no mention because they have evoked no comment on methods. The references given are not necessarily to first editions. Generally speaking, it has been the prefaces to translations that have yielded material, and such prefaces, especially during the Elizabethan period, are likely to be included or omitted in different editions for no very clear reasons. Quotations have been modernized, except in the case of Middle English verse, where the original form has been kept for the sake of the metre.

The history of the theory of translation is by no means a record of easily distinguishable, orderly progression. It shows an odd lack of continuity. Those who give rules for translation ignore, in the great majority of cases, the contribution of their predecessors and contemporaries. Towards the beginning of Elizabeth's reign a small group of critics bring to the problems of the translator both technical scholarship and alert, original minds, but apparently the new and significant ideas which they offer have little or no effect on the general course of theory. Again, Tytler, whose *Essay on the Principles on Translation*, published towards the end of the eighteenth century, may with some reason claim to be the first detailed discussion of the questions involved, declares that, with a few exceptions, he has "met with nothing that has been written professedly on the subject," a statement showing a surprising disregard for the elaborate prefaces that accompanied the translations of his own century.

This lack of consecutiveness in criticism is probably partially accountable for the slowness with which translators attained the power to put into words, clearly and unmistakably, their aims and methods. Even if one were to leave aside the childishly vague comment of medieval writers and the awkward attempts of Elizabethan translators to describe their processes, there would still remain in the modern period much that is careless or misleading. The very term "translation" is long in defining itself; more difficult terms, like "faithfulness" and "accuracy," have widely different meanings with different writers. The various kinds of literature are often treated in the mass with little attempt at discrimination between them, regardless of the fact that the problems of the translator vary with the character of his original. Tytler's book, full of interesting detail as it is, turns from prose to verse, from lyric to epic, from ancient to modern, till the effect it leaves on the reader is fragmentary and confusing.

Moreover, there has never been uniformity of opinion with regard to the aims and methods of translation. Even in the age of Pope, when, if ever, it was safe to be dogmatic and when the theory of translation seemed safely on the way to become standardized, one still hears the voices of a few recalcitrants, voices which become louder and more numerous as the century advances; in the nineteenth century the most casual survey discovers conflicting views on matters of fundamental importance to the translator. Who are to be the readers, who the judges, of a translation are obviously questions of primary significance to both translator and critic, but they are questions which have never been authoritatively settled. When, for example, Caxton in the fifteenth century uses the "curious" terms which he thinks will appeal to a clerk or a noble gentleman, his critics complain because the common people cannot understand his words. A similar situation appears in modern times when Arnold lays down the law that the judges of an English version of Homer must be "scholars, because scholars alone have the means of really judging him," and Newman replies that "scholars are the tribunal of Erudition, but of Taste the educated but unlearned public must be the only rightful judge."

Again, critics have been hesitant in defining the all-important term "faithfulness." To one writer fidelity may imply a reproduction of his original as nearly as possible word for word and fine for line; to another it may mean an attempt to carry over into English the spirit of the original, at the sacrifice, where necessary, not only of the exact words but of the exact substance of his source. The one extreme is likely to result in an awkward, more or less unintelligible version; the other, as illustrated, for example, by Pope's *Homer*, may give us a work so modified by the personality of the translator or by the prevailing taste of his time as to be almost a new creation. But while it is easy to point out the defects of the two methods, few critics have had the courage to give fair consideration to both possibilities; to treat the two aims, not as mutually exclusive, but as complementary; to realize that the spirit and the letter may be not two but one. In the sixteenth century Sir Thomas North translated from the French Amyot's wise observation: "The office of a fit translator consisteth not only in the faithful expressing of his author's meaning, but also in a certain resembling and shadowing forth of the form of his style and manner of his speaking"; but few English critics, in the period under our consideration, grasped thus firmly the essential connection between thought and style and the consequent responsibility of the translator.

Yet it is those critics who have faced all the difficulties boldly, and who have urged upon the translator both due regard for the original and due regard for English literary standards who have made the most valuable contributions to theory. It is much easier to set the standard of translation low, to settle matters as does Mr. Chesterton in his casual disposition of Fitzgerald's *Omar*: "It is quite clear that Fitzgerald's work is much too good to be a good translation." We can, it is true, point to few realizations of the ideal theory, but in approaching a literature which possesses the English Bible, that marvelous union of faithfulness to source with faithfulness to the genius of the English language, we can scarcely view the problem of translation thus hopelessly.

The most stimulating and suggestive criticism, indeed, has come from men who have seen in the very difficulty of the situation opportunities for achievement. "While the more cautious grammarian has ever been doubtful of the quality of the translator's English, fearful of the introduction of foreign words, foreign idioms, to the men who have cared most about the destinies of the vernacular,—men like Caxton, More, or Dryden,—translation has appeared not an enemy to the mother tongue, but a means of enlarging and clarifying it. In the time of Elizabeth the translator often directed his appeal more especially to those who loved their country's language and wished to see it become a more adequate medium of expression. That he should, then, look upon translation as a promising experiment, rather than a doubtful compromise, is an essential characteristic of the good critic.

The necessity for open-mindedness, indeed, in some degree accounts for the tentative quality in so much of the theory of translation. Translation fills too large a place, is too closely connected with the whole course of literary development, to be disposed of easily. As each succeeding period has revealed new fashions in literature, new avenues of approach to the reader, there have been new translations and the theorist has had to reverse or revise the opinions bequeathed to him from a previous period. The theory of translation cannot be reduced to a rule of thumb; it must again and again be modified to include new facts. Thus regarded it becomes a vital part of our literary history, and has significance both for those who love the English language and for those who love English literature.

In conclusion, it remains only to mention a few of my many obligations. To the libraries of Princeton and Harvard as well as Columbia University I owe access to much useful material. It is a pleasure to acknowledge my indebtedness to Professors Ashley H. Thorndike and William W. Lawrence and to Professor William H. Hulme of Western Reserve University for helpful criticism and suggestions. In especial I am deeply grateful to Professor George Philip Krapp, who first suggested this study and who has given me constant encouragement and guidance throughout its course.

April, 1919.

I. The Medieval Period

From the comment of Anglo-Saxon writers one may derive a not inadequate idea of the attitude generally prevailing in the medieval period with regard to the treatment of material from foreign sources. Suggestive statements appear in the prefaces to the works associated with the name of Alfred. One method of translation is employed in producing an English version of Pope Gregory's *Pastoral Care*. "I began," runs the preface, "among other various and manifold troubles of this kingdom, to translate into English the book which is called in Latin *Pastoralis*, and in English *Shepherd's Book*, sometimes word by word, and sometimes according to the sense."[1] A similar practice is described in the *Proem* to *The Consolation of Philosophy* of Boethius. "King Alfred was the interpreter of this book, and turned it from book Latin into English, as it is now done. Now he set forth word by word, now sense from sense, as clearly and intelligently as he was able."[2] The preface to *St. Augustine's Soliloquies*, the beginning of which, unfortunately, seems to be lacking, suggests another possible treatment of borrowed material. "I gathered for myself," writes the author, "cudgels, and stud-shafts, and horizontal shafts, and helves for each of the tools that I could work with, and bow-timbers and bolt-timbers for every work that I could perform, the comeliest trees, as many as I could carry. Neither came I with a burden home, for it did not please me to bring all the wood back, even if I could bear it. In each tree I saw something that I needed at home; therefore I advise each one who can, and has many wains, that he direct his steps to the same wood where I cut the stud-shafts. Let him fetch more for himself, and load his wains with fair beams, that he may wind many a neat wall, and erect many a rare house, and build a fair town, and

[1]Trans. in *Gregory's Pastoral Care*, ed. Sweet, E. E. T. S., p. 7.

[2]Trans. in *King Alfred's Version of the Consolations of Boethius*, trans. Sedgefield, 1900.

therein may dwell merrily and softly both winter and summer, as I have not yet done."[3]

Aelfric, writing a century later, develops his theories in greater detail. Except in the *Preface to Genesis*, they are expressed in Latin, the language of the lettered, a fact which suggests that, unlike the translations themselves, the prefaces were addressed to readers who were, for the most part, opposed to translation into the vernacular and who, in addition to this, were in all probability especially suspicious of the methods employed by Aelfric. These methods were strongly in the direction of popularization. Aelfric's general practice is like that of Alfred. He declares repeatedly[4] that he translates sense for sense, not always word for word. Furthermore, he desires rather to be clear and simple than to adorn his style with rhetorical ornament.[5] Instead of unfamiliar terms, he uses "the pure and open words of the language of this people."[6] In connection with the translation of the Bible he lays down the principle that Latin must give way to English idiom.[7] For all these things Aelfric has definite reasons. Keeping always in mind a clear conception of the nature of his audience, he does whatever seems to him necessary to make his work attractive and, consequently, profitable. Preparing his *Grammar* for "tender youths," though he knows that words may be interpreted in many ways, he follows a simple method of interpretation in order that the book may not become tiresome.[8] The *Homilies*,

---

[3]Trans, in Hargrove, *King Alfred's Old English Version of St. Augustine's Soliloquies*, 1902, pp. xliii-xliv.

[4]Latin Preface of the *Catholic Homilies I*, Latin Preface of the *Lives of the Saints*, Preface of *Pastoral Letter for Archbishop Wulfstan*. All of these are conveniently accessible in White, *Aelfric*, Chap. XIII.

[5]Latin Preface to *Homilies II*.

[6]*Ibid.*

[7]*Preface to Genesis.*

[8]Latin Preface of the *Grammar*.

intended for simple people, are put into simple English, that they may more easily reach the hearts of those who read or hear.[9] This popularization is extended even farther. Aelfric explains[10] that he has abbreviated both the *Homilies*[11] and the *Lives of the Saints*,[12] again of deliberate purpose, as appears in his preface to the latter: "Hoc sciendum etiam quod prolixiores passiones breuiamus verbis non adeo sensu, ne fastidiosis ingeratur tedium si tanta prolixitas erit in propria lingua quanta est in latina."

Incidentally, however, Aelfric makes it evident that his were not te only theories of translation which the period afforded. In the preface to the first collection of *Homilies* he anticipates the disapproval of those who demand greater closeness in following originals. He recognizes the fact that his translation may displease some critics "quod non semper verbum ex verbo, aut quod breviorem explicationem quam tractatus auctorum habent, sive non quod per ordinem ecclesiastici ritus omnia Evangelia percurrimus." The *Preface to Genesis* suggests that the writer was familiar with Jerome's insistence on the necessity for unusual faithfulness in translating the Bible.[13] Such comment implies a mind surprisingly awake to the problems of translation.

The translator who left the narrow path of word for word reproduction might, in this early period, easily be led into greater deviations from source, especially if his own creative ability came into play. The preface to *St. Augustine's Soliloquies* quoted above carries with it a stimulus, not only to translation

---

[9]Latin Preface to *Homilies I.*

[10]In the selections from the Bible various passages, e.g., genealogies, are omitted without comment.

[11]Latin Preface to *Homilies I.*

[12]Latin Preface.

[13]For further comment, see Chapter II.

or compilation, but to work like that of Caedmon or Cynewulf, essentially original in many respects, though based, in the main, on material already given literary shape in other languages. Both characteristics are recognized in Anglo-Saxon comment. Caedmon, according to the famous passage in Bede, "all that he could learn by hearing meditated with himself, and, as a clean animal ruminating, turned into the sweetest verse."[14] Cynewulf in his *Elene*, gives us a remarkable piece of author's comment[15] which describes the action of his own mind upon material already committed to writing by others. On the other hand, it may be noted that the *Andreas*, based like the *Elene* on a single written source, contains no hint that the author owes anything to a version of the story in another language.[16]

In the English literature which developed in course of time after the Conquest the methods of handling borrowed material were similar in their variety to those we have observed in Anglo-Saxon times. Translation, faithful except for the omission or addition of certain passages, compilation, epitome, all the gradations between the close rendering and such an individual creation as Chaucer's *Troilus and Criseyde*, are exemplified in the works appearing from the thirteenth century on. When Lydgate, as late as the fifteenth century, describes one of the processes by which literature is produced, we are reminded of Anglo-Saxon comment. "Laurence,"[17] the poet's predecessor in translating Boccaccio's *Falls of Princes*, is represented as

> In his Prologue affirming of reason,
> That artificers having exercise,

---

[14] Trans. in Thorpe, *Caedmon's Metrical Pharaphrase*, London, 1832, p. XXV.

[15] Ll. 1238 ff. For trans. see *The Christ of Cynewulf*, ed. Cook, pp. xlvi-xlviii.

[16] Cf. comment on l. 1, in Introduction to *Andreas*, ed. Krapp, 1906, p. lii: "The Poem opens with the conventional formula of the epic, citing tradition as the source of the story, though it is all plainly of literary origin."

[17] I.e. Laurent de Premierfait.

May chaunge & turne by good discretion
Shapes & formes, & newly them devise:
As Potters whiche to that craft entende
Breake & renue their vessels to amende.

…

And semblably these clerkes in writing
Thing that was made of auctours them beforn
They may of newe finde & fantasye:
Out of olde chaffe trye out full fayre corne,
Make it more freshe & lusty to the eye,
Their subtile witte their labour apply,
With their colours agreable of hue,
To make olde thinges for to seme newe.[18]

The great majority of these Middle English works contain
within themselves no clear statement as to which of the many
possible methods have been employed in their production. As
in the case of the Anglo-Saxon *Andreas,* a retelling in English
of a story already existing in another language often presents
itself as if it were an original composition. The author who
puts into the vernacular of his country a French romance may
call it "my tale." At the end of *Launfal,* a version of one of the
lays of Marie de France, appears the declaration, "Thomas
Chestre made this tale."[19] The terms used to characterize literary productions and literary processes often have not their
modern connotation. "Translate" and "translation" are applied very loosely even as late as the sixteenth century. *The
Legend of Good Women* names *Troilus and Criseyde* beside *The
Romance of the Rose* as "translated" work.[20] Osbern Bokenam,
writing in the next century, explains that he obtained the material for his legend of St. Margaret "the last time I was in

---

[18]*Bochas' Falls of Princes,* 1558.

[19]Ed. Ritson, ll. 1138-9.

[20]A version, ll. 341-4. Cf. Puttenham, "… many of his books be but bare translations
out of the Latin and French … as his books of *Troilus and Cresseid,* and the *Ro-
mant of the Rose,*" Gregory Smith, *Elizabethan Critical Essays,* ii, 64.

Italy, both by scripture and eke by mouth," but he still calls the work a "translation."[21] Henry Bradshaw, purposing in 1513 to "translate" into English the life of St. Werburge of Chester, declares,

> Unto this rude werke myne auctours these shalbe:
> Fyrst the true legende and the venerable Bede,
> Mayster Alfrydus and Wyllyam Malusburye,
> Gyrarde, Polychronicon, and other mo in deed.[22]

Lydgate is requested to translate the legend of St. Giles "after the tenor only"; he presents his work as a kind of "brief compilation," but he takes no exception to the word "translate."[23] That he should designate his St. Margaret, a fairly close following of one source, a "compilation,"[24] merely strengthens the belief that the terms "translate" and "translation" were used synonymously with various other words. Osbern Bokenam speaks of the "translator" who "compiled" the legend of St. Christiana in English;[25] Chaucer, one remembers, "translated" Boethius and "made" the life of St. Cecilia.[26]

To select from this large body of literature, "made," "compiled," "translated," only such works as can claim to be called, in the modern sense of the word, "translations" would be a difficult and unprofitable task. Rather one must accept the situation as it stands and consider the whole mass of such writings as appear, either from the claims of their authors or on the authority of modern scholarship, to be of secondary origin. "Translations" of this sort are numerous. Chaucer in his own

---

[21] *Osbern Bokenam's Legenden*, ed. Horstmann, 1883, ll. 108-9, 124.

[22] *The Life of St. Werburge*, E. E. T. S., ll. 94. 127-130.

[23] *Minor Poems of Lydgate*, E. E. T. S., Legend of St. Gyle, ll. 9-10, 27-32.

[24] *Ibid.*, Legend of St. Margaret, l. 74.

[25] *St. Christiana*, l. 1028.

[26] *Legend of Good Women*, ll. 425-6.

time was reckoned "grant translateur."[27] Of the books which Caxton a century later issued from his printing press a large proportion were English versions of Latin or French works. Our concern, indeed, is with the larger and by no means the least valuable part of the literature produced during the Middle English period.

The theory which accompanies this nondescript collection of translations is scattered throughout various works, and is somewhat liable to misinterpretation if taken out of its immediate context. Before proceeding to consider it, however, it is necessary to notice certain phases of the general literary situation which created peculiar difficulties for the translator or which are likely to be confusing to the present-day reader. As regards the translator, existing circumstances were not encouraging. In the early part of the period he occupied a very lowly place. As compared with Latin, or even with French, the English language, undeveloped and unstandardized, could make its appeal only to the unlearned. It had, in the words of a thirteenth-century translator of Bishop Grosseteste's *Castle of Love*, "no savor before a clerk."[28] Sometimes, it is true, the English writer had the stimulus of patriotism. The translator of *Richard Cœur de Lion* feels that Englishmen ought to be able to read in their own tongue the exploits of the English hero. The *Cursor Mundi* is translated

> In to Inglis tong to rede
> For the love of Inglis lede,
> Inglis lede of Ingland.[29]

But beyond this there was little to encourage the translator. His audience, as compared with the learned and the refined, who read Latin and French, was ignorant and undiscriminat-

---

[27]See the ballade by Eustache Deschamps, quoted in Chaucer, *Works*, ed. Morris, vol. 1, p. 82.

[28]*Minor Poems of the Vernon MS*, Pt. 1, E. E. T. S., The Castle of Love, l. 72.

[29]E. E. T. S., *Cotton Vesp. MS.* ll. 233-5.

ing; his crude medium was entirely unequal to reproducing what had been written in more highly developed languages. It is little wonder that in these early days his English should be termed "dim and dark." Even after Chaucer had showed that the despised language was capable of grace and charm, the writer of less genius must often have felt that beside the more sophisticated Latin or French, English could boast but scanty resources.

There were difficulties and limitations also in the choice of material to be translated. Throughout most of the period literature existed only in manuscript; there were few large collections in any one place; travel was not easy. Priests, according to the prologue to Mirk's *Festial*, written in the early fifteenth century, complained of "default of books." To aspire, as did Chaucer's Clerk, to the possession of "twenty books" was to aspire high. Translators occasionally give interesting details regarding the circumstances under which they read and translated. The author of the life of St. Etheldred of Ely refers twice, with a certain pride, to a manuscript preserved in the abbey of Godstow which he himself has seen and from which he has drawn some of the facts which he presents. The translator of the alliterative romance of *Alexander* "borrowed" various books when he undertook his English rendering.[30] Earl Rivers, returning from the Continent, brought back a manuscript which had been lent him by a French gentleman, and set about the translation of his *Dictes and Sayings of the Old Philosophers*.[31] It is not improbable that there was a good deal of borrowing, with its attendant inconveniences. Even in the sixteenth century Sir Thomas Elyot, if we may believe his story, was hampered by the laws of property. He became interested in the acts and wisdom of Alexander Severus, "which book," he says, "was first written in the Greek tongue by his secretary Eucolpius and by good chance was lent unto me by a gentle-

---

[30] E. E. T. S., I. 457.

[31] See *Cambridge History of English Literature*, v. 2, p. 313.

man of Naples called Padericus. In reading whereof I was marvelously ravished, and as it hath ever been mine appetite, I wished that it had been published in such a tongue as more men might understand it. Wherefore with all diligence I endeavored myself whiles I had leisure to translate it into English: albeit I could not so exactly perform mine enterprise as I might have done, if the owner had not importunately called for his book, whereby I was constrained to leave some part of the work untranslated."[32] William Paris—to return to the earlier period—has left on record a situation which stirs the imagination. He translated the legend of St. Cristine while a prisoner in the Isle of Man, the only retainer of his unfortunate lord, the Earl of Warwick, whose captivity he chose to share.

> He made this lyfe in ynglishe soo,
> As he satte in prison of stone,
> Ever as he myghte tent therto
> Whane he had his lordes service done.[33]

One is tempted to let the fancy play on the combination of circumstances that provided him with the particular manuscript from which he worked. It is easy, of course, to emphasize overmuch the scarcity and the inaccessibility of texts, but it is obvious that the translator's choice of subject was largely conditioned by opportunity. He did not select from the whole range of literature the work which most appealed to his genius. It is a far cry from the Middle Ages to the seventeenth century, with its stress on individual choice. Roscommon's advice,

> Examine how your humour is inclined,
> And what the ruling passion of your mind;
> Then seek a poet who your way does bend,
> And choose an author as you choose a friend,

---

[32]Preface to *The Image of Governance*, 1549.

[33]*Sammlung Altenglischer Legenden*, ed. Horstmann, *Christine*, ll. 517-20.

seems absurd in connection with the translator who had to choose what was within his reach, and who, in many cases, could not sit down in undisturbed possession of his source.

The element of individual choice was also diminished by the intervention of friends and patrons. In the fifteenth century, when translators were becoming communicative about their affairs, there is frequent reference to suggestion from without. Allowing for interest in the new craft of printing, there is still so much mention in Caxton's prefaces of commissions for translation as to make one feel that "ordering" an English version of some foreign book had become no uncommon thing for those who owned manuscripts and could afford such commodities as translations. Caxton's list ranges from *The Fayttes of Armes*, translated at the request of Henry VII from a manuscript lent by the king himself, to *The Mirror of the World*, "translated ... at the request, desire, cost, and dispense of the honorable and worshipful man, Hugh Bryce, alderman and citizen of London."[34]

One wonders also how the source, thus chosen, presented itself to the translator's conception. His references to it are generally vague or confused, often positively misleading. Yet to designate with any definiteness a French or Latin text was no easy matter. When one considers the labor that, of later years, has gone to the classification and identification of old manuscripts, the awkward elaboration of nomenclature necessary to distinguish them, the complications resulting from missing pages and from the undue liberties of copyists, one realizes something of the position of the medieval translator. Even categories were not forthcoming for his convenience. The religious legend of *St. Katherine of Alexandria* is derived from "chronicles";[35] the moral tale of *The Incestuous Daughter* has its source in "romance";[36] Grosseteste's allegory, *The Castle of Love*, is presented as "a romance of English ... out of a ro-

---

[34]Preface, E. E. T. S.

[35]Capgrave, *St. Katherine of Alexandria*, E. E. T. S., Bk. 3, l. 21.

mance that Sir Robert, Bishop of Lincoln, made."[37] The translator who explained "I found it written in old hand" was probably giving as adequate an account of his source as truth would permit.

Moreover, part of the confusion had often arisen before the manuscript came into the hands of the English translator. Often he was engaged in translating something that was already a translation. Most frequently it was a French version of a Latin original, but sometimes its ancestry was complicated by the existence or the tradition of Greek or Hebrew sources. The medieval Troy story, with its list of authorities, Dictys, Dares, Guido delle Colonne—to cite the favorite names—shows the situation in an aggravated form. In such cases the earlier translator's blunders and omissions in describing his source were likely to be perpetuated in the new rendering.

Such, roughly speaking, were the circumstances under which the translator did his work. Some of his peculiar difficulties are, approached from another angle, the difficulties of the present-day reader. The presence of one or more intermediary versions, a complication especially noticeable in England as a result of the French occupation after the Conquest, may easily mislead us. The originals of many of our texts are either non-extant or not yet discovered, but in cases where we do possess the actual source which the English writer used, a disconcerting situation often becomes evident. What at first seemed to be the English translator's comment on his own treatment of source is frequently only a literal rendering of a comment already present in his original. It is more convenient to discuss the details of such cases in another context, but any general approach to the theory of translation in Middle English literature must include this consideration. If we are not in possession of the exact original of a translation, our conclusions must nearly always be discounted by the possibility that not only

---

[36]In *Altenglische Legenden, Neue Folge*, I. 45.

[37]*Minor Poems of the Vernon MS.* Pt. 1, Appendix, p. 407.

the subject matter but the comment on that subject matter came from the French or Latin source. The pronoun of the first person must be regarded with a slight suspicion. "I" may refer to the Englishman, but it may also refer to his predecessor who made a translation or a compilation in French or Latin. "Compilation" suggests another difficulty. Sometimes an apparent reference to source is only an appeal to authority for the confirmation of a single detail, an appeal which, again, may be the work of the English translator, but may, on the other hand, be the contribution of his predecessor. A fairly common situation, for example, appears in John Capgrave's *Life of St. Augustine*, produced, as its author says, in answer to the request of a gentlewoman that he should "translate her truly out of Latin the life of St. Augustine, great doctor of the church." Of the work, its editor, Mr. Munro, says, "It looks at first sight as though Capgrave had merely translated an older Latin text, as he did in the *Life of St. Gilbert*; but no Latin life corresponding to our text has been discovered, and as Capgrave never refers to "myn auctour," and always alludes to himself as handling the material, I incline to conclude that he is himself the original composer, and that his reference to translation signifies his use of Augustine's books, from which he translates whole passages."[38] In a case like this it is evidently impossible to draw dogmatic conclusions. It may be that Capgrave is using the word "translate" with medieval looseness, but it is also possible that some of the comment expressed in the first person is translated comment, and the editor adds that, though the balance of probability is against it, "it is still possible that a Latin life may have been used." Occasionally, it is true, comment, is stamped unmistakably as belonging to the English translator. The translator of a *Canticum de Creatione* declares that there were

> —fro the incarnacioun of Jhesu
> Til this rym y telle yow

---

[38]Introduction to Capgrave, *Lives of St. Augustine and St. Gilbert of Sempringham*, E. E. T. S.

> Were turned in to englisch,
> A thousand thre hondred & seventy
> And fyve yere witterly.
> Thus in bok founden it is.[39]

Such inquestionably *English* additions are, unfortunately, rare and the situation remains confused.

But this is not the only difficulty which confronts the reader. He searches with disappointing results for such general and comprehensive statements of the medieval translator's theory as may aid in the interpretation of detail. Such statements are few, generally late in date, and, even when not directly translated from a predecessor, are obviously repetitions of the conventional rule associated with the name of Jerome and adopted in Anglo-Saxon times by Alfred and Aelfric. An early fifteenth-century translator of the *Secreta Secretorum*, for example, carries over into English the preface of the Latin translator: "I have translated with great travail into open understanding of Latin out of the language of Araby ... sometimes expounding letter by letter, and sometimes understanding of understanding, for other manner of speaking is with Arabs and other with Latin."[40] Lydgate makes a similar statement:

> I wyl translate hyt sothly as I kan,
> After the lettre, in ordre effectuelly.
> Thogh I not folwe the wordes by & by,
> I schal not faille touching the substance.[41]

Osbern Bokenam declares that he has translated

---

[39] *Sammlung Altenglischer Legenden*, p. 138, ll. 1183-8.

[40] *Three Prose Versions of Secreta Secretorum*, E. E. T. S., Epistle Dedicatory to second.

[41] *The Pilgrimage of the Life of Man*, E. E. T. S.

> Not wurde for wurde—for that ne may be
> In no translation, aftyr Jeromys decree—
> But fro sentence to sentence.[42]

There is little attempt at the further analysis which would give this principle fresh significance. The translator makes scarcely any effort to define the extent to which he may diverge from the words of his original or to explain why such divergence is necessary. John de Trevisa, who translated so extensively in the later fourteenth century, does give some account of his methods, elementary, it is true, but honest and individual. His preface to his English prose version of Higden's *Polychronicon* explains: "In some place I shall set word for word, and active for active, and passive for passive, a-row right as it standeth, without changing of the order of words. But in some place I must change the order of words, and set active for passive and again-ward. And in some place I must set a reason for a word and tell what it meaneth. But for all such changing the meaning shall stand and not be changed."[43] An explanation like this, however, is unusual.

Possibly the fact that the translation was in prose affected Trevisa's theorizing. A prose rendering could follow its original so closely that it was possible to describe the comparatively few changes consequent on English usage. In verse, on the other hand, the changes involved were so great as to discourage definition. There are, however, a few comments on the methods to be employed in poetical renderings. According to the *Proem* to the *Boethius*, Alfred, in the Anglo-Saxon period, first translated the book "from Latin into English prose," and then "wrought it up once more into verse, as it is now done."[44] At the very beginning of the history of Middle English litera-

---

[42]*Osbern Bokenam's Legenden, St. Agnes*, ll. 680-2.

[43]*Epistle of Sir John Trevisa*, in Pollard, *Fifteenth Century Prose and Verse*, p. 208.

[44]In Sedgefield, *King Alfred's Version of Boethius.*

ture Orm attacked the problem of the verse translation very directly. He writes of his Ormulum:

> Icc hafe sett her o thiss boc
> Amang Godspelles wordess,
> All thurrh me sellfenn, manig word
> The rime swa to fillenn.[45]

Such additions, he says, are necessary if the readers are to understand the text and if the metrical form is to be kept.

> Forr whase mot to laewedd folle
> Larspell off Goddspell tellenn,
> He mot wel ekenn manig word
> Amang Godspelless Wordess.
> & icc ne mihhte nohht min ferrs
> Ayy withth Godspelless wordess
> Wel fillenn all, & all forrthi
> Shollde icc wel offte nede
> Amang Godspelless wordess don
> Min word, min ferrs to fillenn.[46]

Later translators, however, seldom followed his lead. There are a few comments connected with prose translations; the translator of *The Book of the Knight of La Tour Landry* quotes the explanation of his author that he has chosen prose rather than verse "for to abridge it, and that it might be better and more plainly to be understood";[47] the Lord in Trevisa's *Dialogue* prefixed to the *Polychronicon* desires a translation in prose, "for commonly prose is more clear than rhyme, more easy and more plain to understand";[48] but apparently the only one of Orm's successors to put into words his consciousness of the

---

[45]Ed. White, 1852, ll. 41-4.

[46]Ll. 55-64.

[47]E. E. T. S., Preface.

[48]Pollard, *ibid.*, p. 208.

complications which accompany a metrical rendering is the author of *The Romance of Partenay*, whose epilogue runs:

> As ny as metre can conclude sentence,
> Cereatly by rew in it have I go.
> Nerehand stafe by staf, by gret diligence,
> Savyng that I most metre apply to;
> The wourdes meve, and sett here & ther so.[49]

What follows, however, shows that he is concerned not so much with the peculiar difficulty of translation as with the general difficulty of "forging" verse. Whether a man employs Latin, French, or the vernacular, he continues,

> Be it in balede, vers, Rime, or prose,
> He most torn and wend, metrely to close.[50]

Of explicit comment on general principles, then, there is but a small amount in connection with Middle English translations. Incidentally, however, writers let fall a good deal of information regarding their theories and methods. Such material must be interpreted with considerable caution, for although the most casual survey makes it clear that generally the translator felt bound to put into words something of his debt and his responsibility to his predecessors, yet one does not know how much significance should attach to this comment. He seldom offers clear, unmistakable information as to his difficulties and his methods of meeting them. It is peculiarly interesting to come upon such explanation of processes as appears at one point in Capgrave's *Life of St. Gilbert*. In telling the story of a miracle wrought upon a sick man, Capgrave writes: "One of his brethren, which was his keeper, gave him this counsel, that he should wind his head with a certain cloth of linen which St. Gilbert wore. I suppose verily," continues the translator, "it was his alb, for mine author here setteth a word 'subucula,' which is both an alb and a shirt, and in the first part of this life

---

[49]E. E. T. S., ll. 6553-7.

[50]Ll. 6565-6.

the same author saith that this holy man wore next his skin no hair as for the hardest, nor linen as for the softest, but he went with wool, as with the mean."[51] Such care for detail suggests the comparative methods later employed by the translators of the Bible, but whether or not it was common, it seldom found its way into words. The majority of writers acquitted themselves of the translator's duty by introducing at intervals somewhat conventional references to source, "in story as we read," "in tale as it is told," "as saith the geste," "in rhyme I read," "the prose says," "as mine author doth write," "as it tells in the book," "so saith the French tale," "as saith the Latin." Tags like these are everywhere present, especially in verse, where they must often have proved convenient in eking out the metre. Whether they are to be interpreted literally is hard to determine. The reader of English versions can seldom be certain whether variants on the more ordinary forms are merely stylistic or result from actual differences in situation; whether, for example, phrases like "as I have heard tell," "as the book says," "as I find in parchment spell" are rewordings of the same fact or represent real distinctions.

One group of doubtful references apparently question the reliability of the written source. In most cases the seeming doubt is probably the result of awkward phrasing. Statements like "as the story doth us both write and mean,"[52] "as the book says and true men tell us,"[53] "but the book us lie,"[54] need have little more significance than the slightly absurd declaration,

> The gospel nul I forsake nought
> *Thaugh* it be written in parchemyn.[55]

---

[51]E. E. T. S., p. 125.

[52]*Altenglische Sammlung, Neue Folge, St. Etheldred Eliensis*, I. 162.

[53]*Sammlung Altenglischer Legenden, Erasmus*, I. 4.

[54]*Ibid., Magdalena*, I. 48.

[55]*Minor Poems of the Vernon MS.*, Pt. 1, *St. Bernard's Lamentation*, II. 21-2.

Occasional more direct questionings incline one, however, to take the matter a little more seriously. The translator of a *Canticum de Creatione*, strangely fabulous in content, presents his material with the words,

> —as we finden in lectrure,
> I not whether it be in holy scripture.[56]

The author of one of the legends of the Holy Cross says,

> This tale, quether hit be il or gode,
> I fande hit writen of the rode.
> Mani tellis diverseli,
> For thai finde diverse stori.[57]

Capgrave, in his legend of *St. Katherine*, takes issue unmistakably with his source.

> In this reknyng myne auctour & I are too:
> ffor he accordeth not wytz cronicles that ben olde,
> But diversyth from hem, & that in many thyngis.
> There he accordeth, ther I him hold;
> And where he diversyth in ordre of theis kyngis,
> I leve hym, & to oder mennys rekenyngis
> I geve more credens whech be-fore hym and me
> Sette alle these men in ordre & degre.[58]

Except when this mistrust is made a justification for divergence from the original, these comments contribute little to our knowledge of the medieval translator's methods and need concern us little. More needful of explanation is the reference which implies that the English writer is not working from a manuscript, but is reproducing something which he has heard read or recounted, or which he has read for himself at some

---

[56]*Sammlung Altenglischer Legenden, Fragment of Canticum de Creatione*, ll. 49-50.

[57]*Legends of the Holy Rood*, E. E. T. S., *How the Holy Cross was found by St. Helena*, ll. 684-7.

[58]E. E. T. S., Bk. 1, ll. 684-91.

time in the past. How is one to interpret phrases like that which introduces the story of *Golagros and Gawain*, "as true men me told," or that which appears at the beginning of *Rauf Coilyear*, "heard I tell"? One explanation, obviously true in some cases, is that such references are only conventional. The concluding lines of *Ywain and Gawin*,

> Of them no more have I heard tell
> Neither in romance nor in spell,[59]

are simply a rough rendering of the French

> Ne ja plus n'en orroiz conter,
> S'an n'i vialt manconge ajoster.[60]

On the other hand, the author of the long romance of *Ipomadon*, which follows its source with a closeness which precludes all possibility of reproduction from memory, has tacked on two references to hearing,[61] not only without a basis in the French but in direct contradiction to Hue de Rotelande's account of the source of his material. In *Emare*, "as I have heard minstrels sing in sawe" is apparently introduced as the equivalent of the more ordinary phrases "in tale as it is told" and "in romance as we read,"[62] the second of which is scarcely compatible with the theory of an oral source.

One cannot always, however, dispose of the reference to hearing so easily. Contemporary testimony shows that literature was often transmitted by word of mouth. Thomas de Cabham mentions the "ioculatores, qui cantant gesta principum et vitam sanctorum";[63] Robert of Brunne complains that those who sing or say the geste of *Sir Tristram* do not repeat the story ex-

---

[59]Ed. Ritson, ll. 4027-8.

[60]*Chevalier au Lyon*, ed. W. L. Holland, 1886, ll. 6805-6.

[61]Ed. Kolbing, 1889, ll. 144, 4514.

[62]E. E. T. S., ll. 319, 405, 216.

[63]See Chambers, *The Medieval Stage*, Appendix G.

actly as Thomas made it.[64] Even though one must recognize the probability that sometimes the immediate oral source of the minstrel's tale may have been English, one cannot ignore the possibility that occasionally a "translated" saint's life or romance may have been the result of hearing a French or Latin narrative read or recited. A convincing example of reproduction from memory appears in the legend of *St. Etheldred of Ely*, whose author recounts certain facts,

> The whiche y founde in the abbey of Godstow y-wis,
> In hure legent as y dude there that tyme rede,

and later presents other material,

> The whiche y say at Hely y-write.[65]

Such evidence makes us regard with more attention the remark in Capgrave's *St. Katherine*,

> —right soo dede I lere
> Of cronycles whiche (that) I saugh last,[66]

or the lines at the end of *Roberd of Cisyle*,

> Al this is write withoute lyghe
> At Rome, to ben in memorye,
> At seint Petres cherche, I knowe.[67]

It is possible also that sometimes a vague phrase like "as the story says," or "in tale as it is told," may signify hearing instead of reading. But in general one turns from consideration of the references to hearing with little more than an increased respect for the superior definiteness which belongs to the mention of the "black letters," the "parchment," "the French book," or "the Latin book."

---

[64]*Chronicle of England*, ed. Furnivall, ll. 93-104.

[65]*Altenglische Legenden, Vita St. Etheldredae Eliensis*, ll. 978-9, 1112.

[66]Bk. 4, ll. 129-130.

[67]*Sammlung Altenglischer Legenden*, ll. 435-7.

Leaving the general situation and examining individual types of literature, one finds it possible to draw conclusions which are somewhat more definite. The metrical romance—to choose one of the most popular literary forms of the period—is nearly always garnished with references to source scattered throughout its course in a manner that awakens curiosity. Sometimes they do not appear at the beginning of the romance, but are introduced in large numbers towards the end; sometimes, after a long series of pages containing nothing of the sort, we begin to come upon them frequently, perhaps in groups, one appearing every few lines, so that their presence constitutes something like a quality of style. For example, in *Bevis of Hamtoun*[68] and *The Earl of Toulouse*[69] the first references to source come between ll. 800 and 900; in *Ywain and Gawin* the references appear at ll. 9, 3209, and 3669;[70] in *The Wars of Alexander*[71] there is a perpetual harping on source, one phrase seeming to produce another.

Occasionally one can find a reason for the insertion of the phrase in a given place. Sometimes its presence suggests that the translator has come upon an unfamiliar word. In *Sir Eglamour of Artois*, speaking of a bird that has carried off a child, the author remarks, "a griffin, saith the book, he hight";[72] in *Partenay*, in an attempt to give a vessel its proper name, the writer says, "I found in scripture that it was a barge."[73] This impression of accuracy is most common in connection with geographical proper names. In *Torrent of Portyn-*

---

[68]E. E. T. S.

[69]Ed. Ritson.

[70]*Ibid.*

[71]E. E. T. S.

[72]*Thornton Romances*, I. 848. (Here the writer is probably confused by the two words *grype* and *griffin*.)

[73]E. E. T. S., I. 1284.

gale we have the name of a forest, "of Brasill saith the book it was"; in *Partonope of Blois* we find "France was named those ilke days Galles, as mine author says,"[74] or "Mine author telleth this church hight the church of Albigis."[75] In this same romance the reference to source accompanies a definite bit of detail, "The French book thus doth me tell, twenty waters he passed full fell."[76] Bevis of Hamtoun kills "forty Sarracens, the French saith."[77] As in the case of the last illustration, the translator frequently needs to cite his authority because the detail he gives is somewhat difficult of belief. In *The Sege of Melayne* the Christian warriors recover their horses miraculously "through the prayer of St. Denys, thus will the chronicle say";[78] in *The Romance of Partenay* we read of a wondrous light appearing about a tomb, "the French maker saith he saw it with eye."[79] Sometimes these phrases suggest that metre and rhyme do not always flow easily for the English writer, and that in such difficulties a stock space-filler is convenient. Lines like those in Chaucer's *Sir Thopas*,

> And so bifel upon a day,
> Forsothe *as I you telle may*
> Sir Thopas wolde outride,

and

> The briddes synge, *it is no nay,*
> The sparhauke and the papejay

may easily be paralleled by passages containing references to source.

---

[74]E. E. T. S., I. 318.

[75]Ll. 6983-4.

[76]Ll. 688-9.

[77]L. 3643.

[78]E. E. T. S., II. 523-4.

[79]L. 6105.

A good illustration from almost every point of view of the significance and lack of significance of the appearance of these phrases in a given context is the version of the Alexander story usually called *The Wars of Alexander*. The frequent references to source in this romance occur in sporadic groups. The author begins by putting them in with some regularity at the beginnings of the *passus* into which he divides his narrative, but, as the story progresses, he ceases to do so, perhaps forgets his first purpose. Sometimes the reference to source suggests accuracy: "And five and thirty, as I find, were in the river drowned."[80] "Rhinoceros, as I read, the book them calls."[81] The strength of some authority is necessary to support the weight of the incredible marvels which the story-teller recounts. He tells of a valley full of serpents with crowns on their heads, who fed, "as the prose tells," on pepper, cloves, and ginger;[82] of enormous crabs with backs, "as the book says," bigger and harder than any common stone or cockatrice scales;[83] of the golden image of Xerxes, which on the approach of Alexander suddenly, "as tells the text," falls to pieces.[84] He often has recourse to an authority for support when he takes proper names from the Latin. "Luctus it hight, the lettre and the line thus it calls."[85] The slayers of Darius are named Besan and Anabras, "as the book tells."[86] On the other hand, the signification of the reference in its context can be shown to be very slight. As was said before, the writer soon forgets to insert it at the beginning of the new *passus*; there are plenty of marvels without any citation of authority to add to their credibility; and though the proper name carries its reference to the Latin, it is usually strangely distorted from its original form. So far

---

[80] E. E. T. S., l. 4734.

[81] L. 4133.

[82] L. 5425.

[83] L. 3894.

[84] L. 2997.

[85] L. 2170.

[86] L. 2428.

as bearing on the immediate context is concerned, most of the references to source have little more meaning than the ordinary tags, "as I you say," "as you may hear," or "as I understand."

Apart, however, from the matter of context, one may make a rough classification of the romances on the ground of these references. Leaving aside the few narratives (e.g. *Sir Percival of Galles*, *King Horn*) which contain no suggestion that they are of secondary origin, one may distinguish two groups. There is, in the first place, a large body of romances which refer in general terms to their originals, but do not profess any responsibility for faithful reproduction; in the second place, there are some romances whose authors do recognize the claims of the original, which is in such cases nearly always definitely described, and frequently go so far as to discuss its style or the style to be adopted in the English rendering. The first group, which includes considerably more than half the romances at present accessible in print, affords a confused mass of references. As regards the least definite of these, one finds phrases so vague as to suggest that the author himself might have had difficulty in identifying his source, phrases where the omission of the article ("in rhyme," "in romance," "in story") or the use of the plural ("as books say," "as clerks tell," "as men us told," "in stories thus as we read") deprives the words of most of their significance. Other references are more definite; the writer mentions "this book," "mine author," "the Latin book," "the French book." If these phrases are to be trusted, we may conclude that the English translator has his text before him; they aid little, however, in identification of that text. The fifty-six references in Malory's *Morte d'Arthur* to "the French book" give no particular clue to discovery of his sources. The common formula, "as the French book says," marks the highest degree of definiteness to which most of these romances attain.

An interesting variant from the commoner forms is the reference to *Rom*, generally in the phrase "the book of Rom," which appears in some of the romances. The explanation that *Rom* is a corruption of *romance* and that *the book of Rom* is simply the book of romance or the book written in the romance language, French, can easily be supported. In the same poem *Rom* alternates with *romance*: "In Rome this geste is chronicled," "as the romance telleth,"[87] "in the chronicles of Rome is the date," "in romance as we read."[88] Two versions of Octavian read, the one "in books of Rome," the other "in books of ryme."[89] On the other hand, there are peculiarities in the use of the word not so easy of explanation. It appears in a certain group of romances, *Octavian, Le Bone Florence of Rome, Sir Eglamour of Artois, Torrent of Portyngale, The Earl of Toulouse*, all of which develop in some degree the Constance story, familiar in *The Man of Law's Tale*. In all of them there is reference to the city of Rome, sometimes very obvious, sometimes slight, but perhaps equally significant in the latter case because it is introduced in an unexpected, unnecessary way. In *Le Bone Florence of Rome* the heroine is daughter of the Emperor of Rome, and, the tale of her wanderings done, the story ends happily with her reinstatement in her own city. Octavian is Emperor of Rome, and here again the happy conclusion finds place in that city. Sir Eglamour belongs to Artois, but he does betake himself to Rome to kill a dragon, an episode introduced in one manuscript of the story by the phrase "as the book of Rome says."[90] Though the scenes of *Torrent of Portyngale* are Portugal, Norway, and Calabria, the Emperor of Rome comes to the wedding of the hero, and Torrent himself is finally chosen Emperor, presumably of Rome. The Earl of Toulouse, in the romance of that name, disguises himself as a monk, and to aid in the illusion some one says of him during his disappearance, "Gone is he to his own land: he dwells with the Pope of

---

[87] *The Earl of Toulouse*, ed. Ritson, ll. 1213, 1197.

[88] Le Bone Florence of Rome, ed. Ritson, ll. 2174, 643.

[89] Ed. Sarrazin, 1885, note on l. 10 of the two versions in Northern dialect.

[90] *Thornton Romances*, note on l. 718.

Rome."[91] The Emperor in this story is Emperor of Almaigne, but his name, strangely enough, is Diocletian. Again, in *Octavian*, one reads in the description of a feast, "there was many a rich geste of Rome and of France,"[92] which suggests a distinction between a geste of Rome and a geste of France. In *Le Bone Florence of Rome* appears the peculiar statement, "Pope Symonde this story wrote. In the chronicles of Rome is the date."[93] In this case the word *Rome* seems to have been taken literally enough to cause attribution of the story to the Pope. It is evident, then, that whether or not *Rome* is a corruption of *romance*, at any rate one or more of the persons who had a hand in producing these narratives must have interpreted the word literally, and believed that the book of Rome was a record of occurrences in the city of Rome.[94] It is interesting to note that in *The Man of Law's Tale*, in speaking of Maurice, the son of Constance, Chaucer introduces a reference to the *Gesta Romanorum*:

> In the old Romayn gestes may men fynde
> Maurice's lyf, I bere it not in mynde.

Such vagueness and uncertainty, if not positive misunderstanding with regard to source, are characteristic of many romances. It is not difficult to find explanations for this. The writer may, as was suggested before, be reproducing a story which he has only heard or which he has read at some earlier time. Even if he has the book before him, it does not necessarily bear its author's name and it is not easy to describe it so that it can be recognized by others. Generally speaking, his references to source are honest, so far as they go, and can be taken at their face value. Even in cases of apparent falsity explanations suggest themselves. There is nearly always the possibility that false or contradictory attributions, as, for example,

---

[91]L. 1150.

[92]Ll. 1275-6.

[93]Ll. 2173-4.

[94]See Miss Rickert's comment in E. E. T. S. edition of *Emare*, p. xlviii.

the mention of "book" and "books" or "the French book" and "the Latin book" as sources of the same romance, are merely stupidly literal renderings of the original. In *The Romance of Partenay*, one of the few cases where we have unquestionably the French original of the English romance, more than once an apparent reference to source in the English is only a close following of the French. "I found in scripture that it was a barge" corresponds with "Je treuve que c'estoit une barge"; "as saith the scripture" with "Ainsi que dient ly escrips";

> For the Cronike doth treteth (sic) this brefly,
> More ferther wold go, mater finde might I

with

> Mais en brief je m'en passeray
> Car la cronique en brief passe.
> Plus déisse, se plus trouvasse.[95]

A similar situation has already been pointed out in *Ywain and Gawin*. The most marked example of contradictory evidence is to be found in *Octavian*, whose author alternates "as the French says" with "as saith the Latin."[96] Here, however, the nearest analogue to the English romance, which contains 1962 lines, is a French romance of 5371 lines, which begins by mentioning the "grans merueilles qui sont faites, et de latin en romanz traites."[97] It is not impossible that the English writer used a shorter version which emphasized this reference to the Latin, and that his too-faithful adherence to source had confusing results. But even if such contradictions cannot be explained, in the mass of undistinguished romances there is scarcely anything to suggest that the writer is trying to give his work a factitious value by misleading references to dignified sources. His faults, as in *Ywain and Gawin*, where the

---

[95]English version, Ll. 1284, 2115, 5718-9; French version, Mellusine, ed. Michel, 1854, ll. 1446, 2302, 6150-2.

[96]Ll. 407, 1359.

[97]Ed. Vollmöller, 1883, ll. 5-6.

name of Chrétien is not carried over from the French, are sins of omission, not commission.

No hard and fast line of division can be drawn between the romances just discussed and those of the second group, with their frequent and fairly definite references to their sources and to their methods of reproducing them. A rough chrono-logical division between the two groups can be made about the year 1400. *William of Palerne*, assigned by its editor to the year 1350, contains a slight indication of the coming change in the claim which its author makes to have accomplished his task "as fully as the French fully would ask."[98] Poems like Chaucer's *Knight's Tale* and *Franklin's Tale* have only the vague references to source of the earlier period, though since they are presented as oral narratives, they belong less obviously to the present discussion. The vexed question of the signification of the references in *Troilus and Criseyde* is outside the scope of this discussion. Superficially considered, they are an odd min-gling of the new and the old. Phrases like "as to myn auctour listeth to devise" (III, 1817), "as techen bokes olde" (III, 91), "as wryten folk thorugh which it is in minde" (IV, 18) suggest the first group. The puzzling references to Lollius have a cer-tain definiteness, and faithfulness to source is implied in lines like:

> And of his song nought only the sentence,
> As writ myn auctour called Lollius,
> But pleynly, save our tonges difference,
> I dar wel seyn, in al that Troilus
> Seyde in his song; lo! every word right thus
> As I shal seyn
> (I, 393-8)

and

> "For as myn auctour seyde, so seye I" (II, 18).

---

[98]E. E. T. S., I. 5522.

But from the beginning of the new century, in the work of men like Lydgate and Caxton, a new habit of comment becomes noticeable.

Less distinguished translators show a similar development. The author of *The Holy Grail*, Harry Lonelich, a London skinner, towards the end of his work makes frequent, if perhaps mistaken, attribution of the French romance to

> ... myn sire Robert of Borron
> Whiche that this storie Al & som
> Owt Of the latyn In to the frensh torned he
> Be holy chirches Comandment sekerle,[99]

and makes some apology for the defects of his own style:

> And I, As An unkonning Man trewly
> Into Englisch have drawen this Story;
> And thowgh that to yow not plesyng It be,
> Yit that ful Excused ye wolde haven Me
> Of my necligence and unkonning.[100]

The Romance of Partenay is turned into English by a writer who presents himself very modestly:

> I not acqueynted of birth naturall
> With frenshe his very trew parfightnesse,
> Nor enpreyntyd is in mind cordiall;
> O word For other myght take by lachesse,
> Or peradventure by unconnyngesse.[101]

He intends, however, to be a careful translator:

> As nighe as metre will conclude sentence,
> Folew I wil my president,
> Ryght as the frenshe wil yiff me evidence,
> Cereatly after myn entent,[102]

---

[99]E. E. T. S., Chap XLVI, ll. 496-9.

[100]Chap. LVI, ll. 521-5.

[101]Ll. 8-12.

[102]Ll. 15-18.

and he ends by declaring that in spite of the impossibility of giving an exact rendering of the French in English metre, he has kept very closely to the original. Sometimes, owing to the shortness of the French "staffes," he has reproduced in one line two lines of the French, but, except for this, comparison will show that the two versions are exactly alike.[103]

The translator of *Partonope of Blois* does not profess such slavish faithfulness, though he does profess great admiration for his source,

> The olde booke full well I-wryted,
> In ffrensh also, and fayre endyted,[104]

and declares himself bound to follow it closely:

> Thus seith myn auctour after whome I write.
> Blame not me: I moste endite
> As nye after hym as ever I may,
> Be it sothe or less I can not say.[105]

However, in the midst of his protestations of faithfulness, he confesses to divergence:

> There-fore y do alle my myghthhe
> To saue my autor ynne sucche wyse
> As he that mater luste devyse,
> Where he makyth grete compleynte
> In french so fayre thatt yt to paynte
> In Englysche tunngge y saye for me
> My wyttys alle to dullet bee.
> He telleth hys tale of sentament
> I vnderstonde noghth hys entent,
> Ne wolle ne besy me to lere.[106]

---

[103]See II. 6581 ff.

[104]Ed. E. E. T. S., II. 600-501.

[105]LI. 7742-6.

[106]LI. 2340-8.

He owns to the abbreviation of descriptive passages, which so many English translators had perpetrated in silence:

> Her bewte dyscry fayne wolde I
> Affter the sentence off myne auctowre,
> Butte I pray yowe of thys grette labowre
> I mote at thys tyme excused be;[107]

> Butte who so luste to here of hur a-raye,
> Lette him go to the ffrensshe bocke,
> That Idell mater I forsoke
> To telle hyt in prose or els in ryme,
> For me thoghte hyt taryed grette tyme.
> And ys a mater full nedless.[108]

One cannot but suspect that this odd mingling of respect and freedom as regards the original describes the attitude of many other translators of romances, less articulate in the expression of their theory.

To deal fairly with many of the romances of this second group, one must consider the relationship between romance and history and the uncertain division between the two. The early chronicles of England generally devoted an appreciable space to matters of romance, the stories of Troy, of Aeneas, of Arthur. As in the case of the romance proper, such chronicles were, even in the modern sense, "translated," for though the historian usually compiled his material from more than one source, his method was to put together long, consecutive passages from various authors, with little attempt at assimilating them into a whole. The distinction between history and romance was slow in arising. The *Morte Arthure* offers within a few lines both "romances" and "chronicles" as authorities for its statements.[109] In Caxton's preface to *Godfrey of Bullogne* the enumeration of the great names of history includes Arthur

---

[107]Ll. 5144-8.

[108]Ll. 6170-6.

[109]Ed. E. E. T. S., ll. 3200, 3218.

and Charlemagne, and the story of Godfrey is designated as "this noble history which is no fable nor feigned thing." Throughout the period the stories of Troy and of Alexander are consistently treated as history, and their redactors frequently state that their material has come from various places. Nearly all the English Troy stories are translations of Guido delle Colonne's *Historia Trojana*, and they take over from their original Guido's long discussion of authorities. The Alexander romances present the same effect of historical accuracy in passages like the following:

> This passage destuted is
> In the French, well y-wis,
> Therefore I have, it to colour
> Borrowed of the Latin author;[110]

> Of what kin he came can I nought find
> In no book that I bed when I began here
> The Latin to this language lelliche to turn.[111]

The assumption of the historian's attitude was probably the largest factor in the development of the habit of expressing responsibility for following the source or for noting divergence from it. Less easy of explanation is the fact that comment on style so frequently appears in this connection. There is perhaps a touch of it even in Layamon's account of his originals, when he approaches his French source: "Layamon began to journey wide over this land, and procured the noble books which he took for authority. He took the English book that Saint Bede made; another he took in Latin that Saint Albin made, and the fair Austin, who brought baptism hither; the third he took, (and) laid there in the midst, that a French clerk made, who was named Wace, who well could write… Layamon laid before him these books, and turned the leaves… pen he took with fingers, and wrote on book skin, and the true

---

[110]*King Alexander*, ed. Weber, 1810, ll. 2199-2202.

[111]Alliterative romance of Alisaunder, E. E. T. S., ll. 456-9.

words set together, and the three books compressed into one."[112] Robert of Brunne, in his *Chronicle of England*, dated as early as 1338, combines a lengthy discussion of style with a clear statement of the extent to which he has used his sources. Wace tells in French

> All that the Latyn spelles,
> ffro Eneas till Cadwaladre;
> this Mayster Wace ther leves he.
> And ryght as Mayster Wace says,
> I telle myn Inglis the same ways.[113]

Pers of Langtoft continues the history;

> & as he says, than say I,[114]

writes the translator. Robert admires his predecessors, Dares, whose "Latyn is feyre to lere," Wace, who "rymed it in Frankis fyne," and Pers, of whose style he says, "feyrer language non ne redis"; but he is especially concerned with his own manner of expression. He does not aspire to an elaborate literary style; rather, he says,

> I made it not forto be praysed,
> Bot at the lewed men were aysed.[115]

Consequently he eschews the difficult verse forms then coming into fashion, "ryme cowee," "straungere," or "enterlace." He does not write for the "disours," "seggers," and "harpours" of his own day, who tell the old stories badly.

> Non tham says as thai tham wrought,
> & in ther sayng it semes noght.[116]

A confusion of pronouns makes it difficult to understand what he considers the fault of contemporary renderings. Possibly it

---

[112]Ed. Madden, 1847.

[113]Ed. Fumivall, 1887, ll. 58-62.

[114]L. 70.

[115]Ll. 83-4.

[116]Ll. 95-6.

is that affectation of an obsolete style to which Caxton refers in the preface to the *Eneydos*. In any case, he himself rejects "straunge Inglis" for "simple speche." Unlike Robert of Brunne, Andrew of Wyntoun, writing at the beginning of the next century, delights in the ornamental style which has added a charm to ancient story.

> Quharfore of sic antiquiteis
> Thei that set haly thare delite
> Gestis or storyis for to write,
> Flurist fairly thare purpose
> With quaynt and curiouse circumstance,
> For to raise hertis in plesance,
> And the heraris till excite
> Be wit or will to do thare delite.[117]

The "antiquiteis" which he has in mind are obviously the tales of Troy. Guido delle Colonne, Homer, and Virgil, he continues, all

> Fairly formyt there tretyss,
> And curiously dytit there storyis.[118]

Some writers, however, did not adopt the elevated style which such subject matter deserves.

> Sum usit bot in plane maner
> Of air done dedis thar mater
> To writ, as did Dares of Frigy,
> That wrait of Troy all the story,
> Bot in till plane and opin style,
> But curiouse wordis or subtile.[119]

Andrew does not attempt to discuss the application of his theory to English style, but he has perhaps suggested the reason why the question of style counted for so much in connection with this pseudo-historical material. In the introduction to

---

[117]Original Chronicle, ll. 6-13.

[118]Ll. 16-17.

[119]Ll. 18-23.

Barbour's *Bruce*, though the point at issue is not translation, there is a similar idea. According to Barbour, a true story has a special claim to an attractive rendering.

> Storyss to rede ar delitabill,
> Supposs that thai be nocht bot fabill;
> Than suld storyss that suthfast wer,
> And thai war said in gud maner,
> Have doubill plesance in heryng.
> The fyrst plesance is the carpyng,
> And the tothir the suthfastness,
> That schawys the thing rycht as it wes.[120]

Lydgate, Wyntoun's contemporary, apparently shared his views. In translating Boccaccio's *Falls of Princes* he dispenses with stylistic ornament.

> Of freshe colours I toke no maner hede.
> But my processe playnly for to lede:
> As me semed it was to me most mete
> To set apart Rethorykes swete.[121]

But when it came to the Troy story, his matter demanded a different treatment. He calls upon Mars

> To do socour my stile to directe,
> And of my penne the tracys to corrects,
> Whyche bareyn is of aureate licour,
> But in thi grace I fynde som favour
> For to conveye it wyth thyn influence.[122]

He also asks aid of Calliope.

> Now of thy grace be helpyng unto me,
> And of thy golde dewe lat the lycour wete
> My dulled breast, that with thyn hony swete

---

[120]Ed. E. E. T. S., Ll. 1-7.

[121]Prologue.

[122]Ed. E. E. T. S., ll. 29-33.

> Sugrest tongis of rethoricyens,
> And maistresse art to musicyens.[123]

Like Wyntoim, Lydgate pays tribute to his predecessors, the clerks who have kept in memory the great deeds of the past

> ... thorough diligent labour,
> And enlumyned with many corious flour
> Of rethorik, to make us comprehend
> The trouthe of al.[124]

Of Guido in particular he writes that he

> ... had in writyng passynge excellence.
> For he enlumyneth by craft & cadence
> This noble story with many fresch colour
> Of rethorik, & many riche flour
> Of eloquence to make it sownde bet
> He in the story hath ymped in and set,
> That in good feyth I trowe he hath no pere.[125]

None of these men point out the relationship between the style of the original and the style to be employed in the English rendering. Caxton, the last writer to be considered in this connection, remarks in his preface to *The Recuyell of the Histories of Troy* on the 'fair language of the French, which was in prose so well and compendiously set and written," and in the prologue to the *Eneydos* tells how he was attracted by the "fair and honest terms and words in French," and how, after writing a leaf or two, he noted that his English was characterized by "fair and strange terms." While it may be that both Caxton and Lydgate were trying to reproduce in English the peculiar quality of their originals, it is more probable that they beautified their own versions as best they could, without feeling it incumbent upon them to make their rhetorical devices correspond with those of their predecessors. Elsewhere Caxton ex-

---

[123]Ll. 54-8.

[124]Ll. 217-20.

[125]Ll. 361-7.

presses concern only for his own language, as it is to be judged by English readers without regard for the qualities of the French. In most cases he characterizes his renderings of romance as "simple and rude"; in the preface to *Charles the Great* he says that he uses "no gay terms, nor subtle, nor new eloquence"; and in the preface to *Blanchardyn and Eglantine* he declares that he does not know "the art of rhetoric nor of such gay terms as now be said in these days and used," and that his only desire is to be understood by his readers. The prologue to the *Eneydos*, however, tells a different story. According to this he has been blamed for expressing himself in, "over curious terms which could not be understood of the common people" and requested to use "old and homely terms." But Caxton objects to the latter as being also unintelligible. "In my judgment," he says, "the common terms that be daily used, are lighter to be understood than the old and ancient English." He is writing, not for the ignorant man, but "only for a clerk and a noble gentleman that feeleth and understandeth in feats of arms, in love, and in noble chivalry." For this reason, he concludes, "in a mean have I reduced and translated this said book into our English, not over rude nor curious, but in such terms as shall be understood, by God's grace, according to the copy." Though Caxton does not avail himself of Wyntoun's theory that the Troy story must be told in "curious and subtle" words, it is probable that, like other translators of his century, he felt the attraction of the new aureate diction while he professed the simplicity of language which existing standards demanded of the translator.

Turning from the romance and the history and considering religious writings, the second large group of medieval productions, one finds the most significant translator's comment associated with the saint's legend, though occasionally the short pious tale or the more abstract theological treatise makes some contribution. These religious works differ from the romances in that they are more frequently based on Latin than on French originals, and in that they contain more deliberate and more repeated references to the audiences to which they have been adapted. The translator does not, like Caxton, write for "a clerk and a noble gentleman"; instead he explains repeatedly that he has striven to make his work understandable to the unlearned, for, as the author of *The Child of Bristow* pertinently remarks,

> The beste song that ever was made
> Is not worth a lekys blade
> But men wol tends ther-tille.[126]

Since Latin enditing is "cumbrous," the translator of *The Blood at Hayles* presents a version in English, "for plainly this the truth will tell";[127] Osbern Bokenam will speak and write "plainly, after the language of Southfolk speech";[128] John Capgrave, finding that the earlier translator of the life of St. Katherine has made the work "full hard… right for the strangeness of his dark language," undertakes to translate it "more openly" and "set it more plain."[129] This conception of the audience, together with the writer's consciousness that even in presenting narrative he is conveying spiritual truths of supreme importance to his readers, probably increases the tendency of the translator to incorporate into his English version such running commentary as at intervals suggests itself to him. He may add a line or two of explanation, of exhortation, or, if he recognizes a quotation from the Scriptures or from the Fathers, he may supply the authority for it. John Capgrave undertakes to translate the life of St. Gilbert "right as I find before me, save some additions will I put thereto which men of that order have told me, and eke other things that shall fall to my mind in the writing which be pertinent to the matter."[130] Nicholas Love puts into English *The Mirror of the Blessed Life of*

---

[126]In *Altenglische Legenden, Neue Folge*, ll. 7-9.

[127]*Ibid.*, ll. 33, 35.

[128]*Osbern Bokenam's Legenden, St. Agnes*, ll. 29-30.

[129]*St. Katherine of Alexandria, Prologue*, ll. 61-2, 232-3, 64.

[130]*Lives of St. Augustine and St. Gilbert, Prologue.*

Jesus Christ, "with more put to in certain parts, and also with drawing out of divers authorities and matters as it seemeth to the writer hereof most speedful and edifying to them that be of simple understanding."[131] Such incidental citation of authority is evident in *St. Paula,* published by Dr. Horstmann side by side with its Latin original.[132] With more simplicity and less display of learning, the translator of religious works sometimes vaguely adduces authority, as did the translator of romances, in connection with an unfamiliar name. One finds such statements as: "Manna, so it is written";[133] "Such a fiend, as the book tells us, is called Incubus";[134] "In the country of Champagne, as the book tells";[135] "Cursates, saith the book, he hight";[136]

> Her body lyeth in strong castylle
> And Bulstene, seith the boke, it hight;[137]

> In the yer of ur lord of hevene
> Four hundred and eke ellevene
> Wandaly the province tok
> Of Aufrike—so seith the bok.[138]

Often, however, the reference to source is introduced apparently at random. On the whole, indeed, the comment which accompanies religious writings does not differ essentially in intelligibility or significance from that associated with romances; its interest lies mainly in the fact that it brings into greater relief tendencies more or less apparent in the other form.

---

[131]Oxford, Clarendon Press, *Prohemium.*

[132]In *Sammlung Altenglischer Legenden.*

[133]*Minor Poems of the Vernon MS., De Festo Corporis Christi,* l. 170.

[134]*Sammlung Altenglischer Legenden, St. Bernard,* ll. 943-4.

[135]*Ibid., Erasmus,* l. 41.

[136]*Altenglische Legenden, Neue Folge, St. Katherine,* p. 243, l. 451.

[137]*Sammlung Altenglischer Legenden, Christine,* ll. 4S9~90.

[138]*Ibid., St. Augustine,* ll. 1137-40.

One of these is the large proportion of borrowed comment. The constant citation of authority in a work such as, for example, *The Golden Legend* was likely to be reproduced in the English with varying degrees of faithfulness. A *Life of St. Augustine*, to choose a few illustrations from many, reproduces the Latin as in the following examples: "as the book telleth us" replaces "dicitur enim"; "of him it is said in Glosarie," "ut dicitur im Glossario"; "in the book of his confessions the sooth is written for the nonce," "ut legitur in libro iii. confessionum."[139] Robert of Brunne's *Handlyng Synne*, as printed by the Early English Text Society with its French original, affords numerous examples of translated references to authority.

> The tale ys wrytyn, al and sum,
> In a boke of Vitas Patrum

corresponds with

> Car en vn liure ai troué
> Qe Vitas Patrum est apelé;
>
> Thus seyth seynt Anselme, that hit wrote
> To thys clerkys that weyl hit wote

with

> Ceo nus ad Seint Ancelme dit
> Qe en la fey fut clerk parfit.

Yet there are variations in the English much more marked than in the last example. "Cum l'estorie nus ad cunté" has become "Yn the byble men mow hyt se"; while for

> En ve liure qe est apelez
> La sume des vertuz & des pechiez

the translator has substituted

> Thys same tale tellyth seynt Bede
> Yn hys gestys that men rede.[140]

---

[139] *Sammlung Altenglischer Legenden, St. Augustine*, ll. 43, 57-8, 128.

[140] Ll. 169-70, 785-6, 2475-6.

This attempt to give the origin of a tale or of a precept more accurately than it is given in the French or the Latin leads sometimes to strange confusion, more especially when a reference to the Scriptures is involved. It was admitted that the Bible was unusually difficult of comprehension and that, if the simple were to understand it, it must be annotated in various ways. Nicholas Love says that there have been written "for lewd men and women... devout meditations of Christ's life more plain in certain parts than is expressed in the gospels of the four evangelists."[141] With so much addition of commentary and legend, it was often hard to tell what was and what was not in Holy Scripture, and consequently while a narrative like *The Birth of Jesus* cites correctly enough the gospels for certain days, of which it gives a free rendering,[142] there are cases of amazing attributions, like that at the end of the legend of *Ypotis*:

> Seynt Jon the Evangelist
> Ede on eorthe with Jhesu Crist,
> This tale he wrot in latin
> In holi bok in parchemin.[143]

After the fifteenth century is reached, the translator of religious works, like the translator of romances, becomes more garrulous in his comment and develops a good deal of interest in English style. As a fair representative of the period we may take Osbern Bokenam, the translator of various saint's legends, a man very much interested in the contemporary development of literary expression. Two qualities, according to Bokenam, characterize his own style; he writes "compendiously" and he avoids "gay speech." He repeatedly disclaims both prolixity and rhetorical ornament. His

---

[141] *Op. cit., Prohemium.*

[142] *Altenglische Legenden, Geburt Jesu*, ll. 493, 527, 715, etc.

[143] *Altenglische Legenden, Neue Folge, Ypotis*, ll. 613-16.

> ... form of procedyng artificyal
> Is in no wyse ner poetical.[144]

He cannot emulate the "first rhetoricians," Gower, Chaucer, and Lydgate; he comes too late; they have already gathered "the most fresh flowers." Moreover the ornamental style would not become him; he does not desire

> ... to have swych eloquence
> As sum curials han, ner swych asperence
> In utteryng of here subtyl conceytys
> In wych oft-tyme ful greth dysceyt is.[145]

To covet the craft of such language would be "great dotage" for an old man like him. Yet like those of Lydgate and Caxton, Bokenam's protestations are not entirely convincing, and in them one catches glimpses of a lurking fondness for the wordiness of fine writing. Though Pallas has always refused to lead him

> Of Thully Rethoryk in-to the motlyd mede,
> Flourys to gadryn of crafty eloquens,[146]

yet he has often prayed her to show him some favor. Elsewhere he finds it necessary to apologize for the brevity of part of his work.

> Now have I shewed more compendiously
> Than it owt have ben this noble pedigree;
> But in that myn auctour I follow sothly,
> And also to eschew prolixite,
> And for my wyt is schort, as ye may se,
> To the second part I wyl me hye.[147]

The conventionality, indeed, of Bokenam's phraseology and of his literary standards and the self-contradictory elements in

---

[144] *Osbern Bokenam's Legenden, St. Margaret*, ll. 84^5.

[145] *Mary Magdalen*, ll. 245-8.

[146] *St. Agnes*, ll. 13-14.

[147] *Op. cit., St. Anne*, ll. 209-14.

his statements leave one with the impression that he has brought little, if anything, that is fresh and individual to add to the theory of translation.

Whether or not the medieval period made progress towards the development of a more satisfactory theory is a doubtful question. While men like Lydgate, Bokenam, and Caxton generally profess to have reproduced the content of their sources and make some mention of the original writers, their comment is confused and indefinite; they do not recognize any compelling necessity for faithfulness; and one sometimes suspects that they excelled their predecessors only in articulateness. As compared with Layamon and Orm they show a development scarcely worthy of a lapse of more than two centuries. There is perhaps, as time goes on, some little advance towards the attainment of modern standards of scholarship as regards confession of divergence from sources. In the early part of the period variations from the original are only vaguely implied and become evident only when the reader can place the English beside the French or Latin. In *Floris and Blancheflor*, for example, a much condensed version of a descriptive passage in the French is introduced by the words, "I ne can tell you how richly the saddle was wrought."[148] The romance of *Arthur* ends with the statement,

> He that will more look,
> Read in the French book,
> And he shall find there
> Things that I leete here.[149]

The *Northern Passion* turns from the legendary history of the Cross to something more nearly resembling the gospel narrative with the exhortation, "Forget not Jesus for this tale."[150] As compared with this, writers like Nicholas Love or John Capgrave are noticeably explicit. Love pauses at various points to

---

[148]E. E. T. S., I. 382.

[149]E. E. T. S., II. 633-6.

[150]E. E. T. S., p. 146, I. 1.

explain that he is omitting large sections of the original;[151] Capgrave calls attention to his interpolations and refers them to their sources.[152] On the other hand, there are constant implications that variation from source may be a desirable thing and that explanation and apology are unnecessary. Bokenam, for example, apologizes rather because *The Golden Legend* does not supply enough material and he must leave out certain things "for ignorance."[153] Caxton says of his *Charles the Great*, "If I had been more largely informed... I had better made it."[154]

On the whole, the greatest merit of the later medieval translators consists in the quantity of their comment. In spite of the vagueness and the absence of originality in their utterances, there is an advantage in their very garrulity. Translators needed to become more conscious and more deliberate in their work; different methods needed to be defined; and the habit of technical discussion had its value, even though the quality of the commentary was not particularly good. Apart from a few conventional formulas, this habit of comment constituted the bequest of medieval translators to their sixteenth-century successors.

---

[151]Op. cit., pp. 100, 115, 300.

[152]*Life of St. Gilbert*, pp. 103, 135, 141.

[153]*Op. cit, St. Katherine*, l. 49.

[154]Preface.

II. The Translation of the Bible

The English Bible took its shape under unusual conditions, which had their share in the excellence of the final result. Appealing, as it did, to all classes, from the scholar, alert for controversial detail, to the unlearned layman, concerned only for his soul's welfare, it had its growth in the vital atmosphere of strong intellectual and spiritual activity. It was not enough that it should bear the test of the scholar's criticism; it must also reach the understanding of Tyndale's "boy that driveth the plough," demands difficult of satisfaction, but conducive theoretically to a fine development of the art of translation. To attain scholarly accuracy combined with practical intelligibility was, then, the task of the translator.

From both angles criticism reached him. Tyndale refers to "my translation in which they affirm unto the lay people (as I have heard say) to be I wot not how many thousand heresies," and continues, "For they which in times past were wont to look on no more scripture than they found in their duns or such like devilish doctrine, have yet now so narrowly looked on my translation that there is not so much as one I therein if it lack a tittle over his head, but they have noted it, and number it unto the ignorant people for an heresy."[155] Tunstall's famous reference in his sermon at Paul's Cross to the two thousand errors in Tyndale's Testament suggests the undiscriminating criticism, addressed to the popular ear and basing its appeal largely on "numbering," of which Tyndale complains. The prohibition of "open reasoning in your open Taverns and Alehouses"[156] concerning the meaning of Scripture, included in the draft of the proclamation for the reading of the Great Bible, also implies that there must have been enough of popular oral discussion to count for something in the shaping of the English Bible. Of the serious comment of more competent

---

[155]*Preface to Genesis*, in Pollard, *Records of the English Bible*, p. 94.

[156]Pollard, p. 266.

judges many records remain, enough to make it clear that, although the real technical problems involved were often obscured by controversy and by the common view that the divine quality of the original made human effort negligible, nevertheless the translator did not lack the stimulus which comes from intelligent criticism and discussion.

The Bible also had an advantage over other translations in that the idea of *progress* towards an accurate version early arose. Unlike the translators of secular works, who frequently boast of the speed with which they have accomplished their tasks, the translators of the Bible constantly mention the long, careful labor which has gone to their undertaking. Tyndale feels in his own work the need for revision, and so far as opportunity serves, corrects and polishes his version. Later translators consciously based their renderings on those of their predecessors. St. Augustine's approval of diversity of translations was cited again and again. Tyndale urges "those that are better seen in the tongues than I" to "put to their hands to amend" any faults they may find in his work.[157] George Joye, his assistant, later his would-be rival, declares that we must learn "to depend not whole on any man's translation."[158] "Every one," says Coverdale, "doth his best to be nighest to the mark. And though they cannot all attain thereto yet shooteth one nigher than another";[159] and again, "Sure I am that there cometh more knowledge and understanding of the scripture by their sundry translations than by all our sophistical doctors. For that one translateth something obscurely in one place, the same translateth another, or else he himself, more manifestly by a more plain vocable."[160] Occasionally the number of experimenters awakened some doubts; Cromwell suggests that the bishops make a "perfect correction";[161] the patent granted him

[157] *Ibid.*, p. 112.

[158] *Ibid.*, p. 187.

[159] *Ibid.*, p. 205.

[160] Cloverdale, *Prologue* to Bible of 1535.
[161] Pollard, p. 196.

for the printing of the Bible advocates one translation since "the frailty of men is such that the diversity thereof may breed and bring forth manyfold inconveniences as when wilful and heady folks shall confer upon the diversity of the said translations";[162] the translators of the version of 1611 have to "answer a third cavil… against us, for altering and amending our translations so oft";[163] but the conception of progress was generally accepted, and finds fit expression in the preface to the Authorized Version: "Yet for all that, as nothing is begun and perfected at the same time, and the later thoughts are thought to be wiser: so, if we building on their foundation that went before us, and being holpen by their labors, do endeavor to make that better which they left so good; no man, we are sure, hath cause to mislike us."[164]

But the English translators had more far-reaching opportunities to profit by the experiences of others. In other countries than England men were engaged in similar labors. The sixteenth century was rich in new Latin versions of the Scriptures. The translations of Erasmus, Beza, Pagniaus, Münster, Étienne, Montanus, and Tremellius had in turn their influence on the English renderings, and Castalio's translation into Ciceronian Latin had at least its share of discussion. There was constant intercourse between those interested in Bible translation in England and on the Continent. English refugees during the persecutions fled across the Channel, and towns such as Worms, Zurich, Antwerp, and Geneva saw the first printing of most of the early English versions of the Scriptures. The Great Bible was set up in Paris. Indeed foreign printers had so large a share in the English Bible that it seemed sometimes advisable to limit their influence. Richard Grafton writes ironically to Cromwell regarding the text of the Bible: "Yea and to make it yet truer than it is, therefore Dutchmen dwelling within this

---

[162]*Ibid.*, p. 259.

[163]*Ibid.*, p. 365.

[164]*Ibid.*, p 360.

realm go about the printing of it, which can neither speak good English, nor yet write none, and they will be both the printers and correctors thereof";[165] and Coverdale and Grafton imply a similar fear in the case of Regnault, the Frenchman, who has been printing service books, when they ask Cromwell that "henceforth he print no more in the English tongue, unless he have an Englishman that is learned to be his corrector."[166] Moreover, versions of the Scriptures in other languages than English were not unknown in England. In 1530 Henry the Eighth was led to prohibit "the having of holy scripture, translated into the vulgar tongues of English, *French*, or *Dutch*."[167] Besides this general familiarity with foreign translations and foreign printers, a more specific indebtedness must be recognized. More's attack on the book "which whoso calleth the New Testament calleth it by a wrong name, except they will call it Tyndale's testament or Luther's testament"[168] is in some degree justified in its reference to German influence. Coverdale acknowledges the aid he has received from "the Dutch interpreters: whom (because to their singular gifts and special diligence in the Bible) I have been the more glad to follow."[169] The preface to the version of 1611 says, "Neither did we think much to consult the translators or commentators, Chaldee, Hebrew, Syrian, Greek, or Latin, no, nor the *Spanish, French, Italian,* or *Dutch*."[170] Doubtless a great part of the debt lay in matters of exegesis, but in his familiarity with so great a number of translations into other languages and with the discussion centering around these translations, it is impossible that the English translator should have failed to obtain suggestions, both practical and theoretical, which applied to translation rather than to interpretation. Comments on the general

---

[165]Pollard, p. 220.

[166]*Ibid.*, p. 239.

[167]*Ibid.*, p. 163.

[168]*Ibid.*, p. 126.

[169]*Ibid.*, p. 203.

[170]*Ibid.*, p. 371.

aims and methods of translation, happy turns of expression in French or German which had their equivalents in English idiom, must frequently have illuminated his difficulties. The translators of the Geneva Bible show a just realization of the truth when they speak of "the great opportunity and occasions which God hath presented unto us in this Church, by reason of so many godly and learned men; and such diversities of translations in divers tongues."[171]

Of the general history of Biblical translations, already so frequently and so adequately treated, only the barest outline is here necessary. The various Anglo-Saxon translations and the Wycliffite versions are largely detached from the main line of development. From Tyndale's translations to the Authorized Version of 1611 the line is surprisingly consecutive, though in the matter of theory an early translator occasionally anticipates views which obtain general acceptance only after a long period of experiment and discussion. Roughly speaking, the theory of translation has as its two extremes, the Roman Catholic and the Puritan positions, while the 1611 version, where its preface commits itself, compromises on the points at issue.

As is to be expected, the most definite statements of the problems involved and of their solution are usually found in the comment of those practically engaged in the work of translation. The widely discussed question whether or not the people should have the Scriptures in the vulgar tongue scarcely ever comes down to the difficulties and possibilities of the actual undertaking. More's lengthy attack on Tyndale's New Testament is chiefly concerned with matters of doctrine. Apart from the prefaces to the various issues of the Bible, the most elaborate discussion of technical matters is Fulke's *Defence of the Sincere and True Translation of the Holy Scriptures into the English Tongue*, a Protestant reply to the claims of the Rhemish translators, published in 1589. Even the more definite comments

---

[171]Pollard, p. 280.

are bound up with a great mass of controversial or hortatory material, so that it is hard to disentangle the actual contribution which is being made to the theory of translation. Sometimes the translator settled vexed questions by using marginal glosses, a method which might make for accuracy but was liable to become cumbrous and confusing. Like the prefaces, the glosses sometimes contained theological rather than linguistic comment, thus proving a special source of controversy. A proclamation of Henry the Eighth forbids the printing or importation of "any books of divine scripture in the English tongue, with any additions in the margin or any prologue… except the same be first viewed, examined, and allowed by the king's highness, or such of his majesty's council, or others, as it shall please his grace to assign thereto, but only the plain sentence and text."[172] The version of 1611 admitted only linguistic comment.

Though the Anglo-Saxon renderings of the Scriptures are for the most part isolated from the main body of translations, there are some points of contact. Elizabethan translators frequently cited the example of the earlier period as an argument in favor of having the Bible in the vulgar tongue. Nor were they entirely unfamiliar with the work of these remote predecessors. Foxe, the martyrologist, published in 1571 an edition of the four gospels in Anglo-Saxon under the patronage of Archbishop Parker. Parker's well-known interest in Old English centered particularly around the early versions of the Scriptures. Secretary Cecil sends the Archbishop "a very ancient Bible written in Latin and old English or Saxon," and Parker in reply comments on "the fair antique writing with the Saxon interpretation."[173] Moreover the slight record which survives suggests that the problems which confronted the Anglo-Saxon translator were not unlike those which met the translator of a later period. Aelfric's theory of translation in

---

[172]Pollard, p. 241.

[173]Strype, *Life of Parker*, London, 1711, p. 536.

general is expressed in the Latin prefaces to the *Homilies of the Anglo-Saxon Church* and the *Lives of the Saints*. Above all things he desires that his work may be clear and readable. Hence he has a peculiar regard for brevity. The *Homilies* are rendered "non garrula verbositate"; the *Lives of the Saints* are abbreviated on the principle that "non semper breuitas sermonem deturpat sed multotiens honestiorem reddit." Clear, idiomatic English is essential even when it demands the sacrifice of verbal accuracy. He presents not word for word but sense for sense, and prefers the "pure and open words of the language of this people," to a more artificial style. His Anglo-Saxon *Preface to Genesis* implies that he felt the need of greater faithfulness in the case of the Bible: "We dare write no more in English than the Latin has, nor change the orders (endebirdnisse)"; but it goes on to say that it is necessary that Latin idiom adapt itself to English idiom.[174]

Apart from Aelfric's prefaces Anglo-Saxon translators of the Scriptures have left no comment on their methods. One of the versions of the Gospels, however, links itself with later translations by employing as preface three of St. Jerome's prologues, among them the *Preface to Eusebius*. References to Jerome's and Augustine's theories of translation are frequent throughout the course of Biblical translation but are generally vague. The *Preface to Eusebius* and the *Epistle to Pammachius* contain the most complete statements of the principles which guided Jerome. Both emphasize the necessity of giving sense for sense rather than word for word, "except," says the latter, "in the case of the Holy Scriptures where even the order of the words is a mystery." This corresponds closely with Aelfric's theory expressed in the preface to the *Lives of the Saints*: "Nec potuimus in ista translatione semper verbum ex verbo transferre, sed tamen sensum ex sensu," and his insistence in the *Preface to Genesis* on a faithfulness which extends even to the *endebirdnisse* or orders.

---

[174]For a further account of Aelfric's theories, see Chapter I.

The principle "word for word if possible; if not, sense for sense" is common in connection with medieval translations, but is susceptible of very different interpretations, as appears sometimes from its context. Richard Rolle's phrasing of the theory in the preface to his translation of the Psalter is: "I follow the letter as much as I may. And where I find no proper English I follow the wit of the words"; but he also makes the contradictory statement, "In this work I seek no strange English, but lightest and commonest, and *such that is most like to the Latin*,"[175] a peculiar conception of the translator's obligation to his own tongue! The Prologue to the second recension of the Wycliffite version, commonly attributed to Purvey, emphasizes, under cover of the same apparent theory, the claims of the vernacular. "The best translating," it runs, "is out of Latin into English, to translate after the sentence, and not only after the words, so that the sentence be as open, either opener, in English as in Latin, … and if the letter may not be sued in the translating, let the sentence be ever whole and open, for the words owe to serve to the intent and sentence."[176] The growing distrust of the Vulgate in some quarters probably accounts in some measure for the translator's attempt to make the meaning if necessary "more true and more open than it is in the Latin." In any case these contrasted theories represent roughly the position of the Roman Catholic and, to some extent, the Anglican party as compared with the more distinctly Protestant attitude throughout the period when the English Bible was taking shape, the former stressing the difficulties of translation and consequently discouraging it, or, when permitting it, insisting on extreme faithfulness to the original; the latter profiting by experiment and criticism and steadily working towards a version which would give due heed not only to the claims of the original but to the genius of the English language.

---

[175] *The Psalter translated by Richard Rolle of Hampole*, ed. Bramley, Oxford, 1884.

[176] Chapter 15, in Pollard, *Fifteenth Century Prose and Verse*.

Regarded merely as theory, however, a statement like the one just quoted obviously failed to give adequate recognition to what the original might justly demand, and in that respect justified the fears of those who opposed translation. The high standard of accuracy set by such critics demanded of the translator an increasing consciousness of the difficulties involved and an increasingly clear conception of what things were and were not permissible. Purvey himself contributes to this end by a definite statement of certain changes which may be allowed the English writer.[177] Ablative absolute or participial constructions may be replaced by clauses of various kinds, "and this will, in many places, make the sentence open, where to English it after the word would be dark and doubtful. Also," he continues, "a relative, *which*, may be resolved into his antecedent with a conjunction copulative, as thus, *which runneth*, and *he runneth*. Also when a word is once set in a reason, it may be set forth as oft as it is understood, either as oft as reason and need ask; and this word *autem* either *vero*, may stand for *forsooth* either for *but*, and thus I use commonly; and sometimes it may stand for *and*, as old grammarians say. Also when rightful construction is letted by relation, I resolve it openly, thus, where this reason, *Dominum formidabunt adversarii ejus*, should be Englished thus by the letter, *the Lord his adversaries shall dread*, I English it thus by resolution, *the adversaries of the Lord shall dread him*; and so of other reasons that be like." In the later period of Biblical translation, when grammatical information was more accessible, such elementary comment was not likely to be committed to print, but echoes of similar technical difficulties are occasionally heard. Tyndale, speaking of the Hebraisms in the Greek Testament, asks his critics to "consider the Hebrew phrase… whose preterperfect tense and present tense is both one, and the future tense is the optative mood also, and the future tense is oft the imperative mood in the active voice and in the passive voice. Likewise person for person, number for number, and interrogation

---

[177]*Prologue*, Chapter 15.

for a conditional, and such like is with the Hebrews a common usage."[178] The men concerned in the preparation of the Bishops' Bible discuss the rendering of tenses in the Psalms. At the beginning of the first Psalm the Bishop of Rochester turns "the preterperfect tense into the present tense; because the sense is too harsh in the preterperfect tense," and the Bishop of Ely advises "the translation of the verbs in the Psalms to be used uniformly in one tense."[179]

Purvey's explanations, however, suggest that his mind is occupied, not merely with details, but with a somewhat larger problem. Medieval translators were frequently disturbed by the fact that it was almost impossible to confine an English version to the same number of words as the Latin. When they added to the number, they feared that they were unfaithful to the original. The need for brevity, for avoiding superfluous words, is especially emphasized in connection with the Bible. Conciseness, necessary for accuracy, is also an admirable quality in itself. Aelfric's approval of this characteristic has already been noted. The metrical preface to Rolle's Psalter reads: "This holy man in expounding, he followeth holy doctors, and in all his Englishing right after the Latin taketh course, and makes it *compendious, short*, good, and profitable." Purvey says, "Men might expound much openlier and *shortlier* the Bible than the old doctors have expounded it in Latin." Besides approving the avoidance of verbose commentary and exposition, critics and translators are always on their guard against the employment of over many words in translation. Tyndale, in his revision, will "seek to bring to compendiousness that which is now translated at the length."[180] In certain cases, he says, English reproduces the Hebrew original more easily than does the Latin, because in Latin the translator must "seek a com-

---

[178]*Prologue to the New Testament*, printed in Matthew's Bible, 1561.

[179]Strype, *Life of Parker*, p. 208.

[180]Pollard, p. 116.

pass."[181] Coverdale finds a corresponding difficulty in turning Latin into English: "The figure called Eclipsis divers times used in the scriptures... though she do garnish the sentence in Latin will not so be admitted in other tongues."[182] The translator of the Geneva New Testament refers to the "Hebrew and Greek phrases, which are strange to render into other tongues, and also short."[183] The preface to the Rhemish Testament accuses the Protestant translators of having in one place put into the text "three words more... than the Greek word doth signify."[184] Strype says of Cheke in a passage chiefly concerned with Cheke's attempt at translation of the Bible, "He brought in a short and expressive way of writing without long and intricate periods,"[185] a comment which suggests that possibly the appreciation of conciseness embraced sentence structure as well as phrasing. As Tyndale suggests, careful revision made for brevity. In Laurence's scheme for correcting his part of the Bishop's Bible was the heading "words superfluous";[186] the preface to the Authorized Version says, "If anything be halting, or *superfluous*, or not so agreeable to the original, the same may be corrected, and the truth set in place."[187] As time went on, certain technical means were employed to meet the situation. Coverdale incloses in brackets words not in the Latin text; the Geneva translators put added words in italics; Fulke criticizes the Rhemish translators for neglecting this device;[188] and the matter is finally settled by its employment in the Authorized Version. Fulke, however, irritated by what he considers a superstitious regard for the number of words in the orig-

---

[181]Preface to *The Obedience of a Christian Man*, in *Doctrinal Treatises*, Parker Society, 1848, p. 390.

[182]Pollard, p. 211.

[183]*Ibid.*, p. 277.

[184]*Ibid.*, p. 306.

[185]*Life of Cheke*, p. 212.

[186]Strype, *Life of Parker*, p. 404.

[187]Pollard, p. 361.

[188]Fulke, *Defence*, Parker Society, p. 552.

inal on the part of the Rhemish translators, puts the whole question on a common-sense basis. He charges his opponents with making "many imperfect sentences... because you will not seem to add that which in translation is no addition, but a true translation."[189] "For to translate out of one tongue into another," he says in another place, "is a matter of greater difficulty than is commonly taken, I mean exactly to yield as much and no more than the original containeth, when the words and phrases are so different, that few are found which in all points signify the same thing, neither more nor less, in divers tongues."[190] And again, "Must not such particles in translation be always expressed to make the sense plain, which in English without the particle hath no sense or understanding. To translate precisely out of the Hebrew is not to observe the number of words, but the perfect sense and meaning, as the phrase of our tongue will serve to be understood."[191]

For the distinguishing characteristics of the Authorized Version, the beauty of its rhythm, the vigor of its native Saxon vocabulary, there is little to prepare one in the comment of its translators or their predecessors. Apparently the faithful effort to render the original truly resulted in a perfection of style of which the translator himself was largely unconscious. The declaration in the preface to the version of 1611 that "niceness in words was always counted the next step to trifling,"[192] and the general condemnation of Castalio's "lewd translation,"[193] point to a respect for the original which made the translator merely a mouthpiece and the English language merely a medium for a divine utterance. Possibly there is to be found in appreciation of the style of the original Hebrew, Greek, or Latin some hint of what gave the English version its peculiar

---

[189]*Defence*, p. 552.

[190]*Ibid.*, p. 97.

[191]*Ibid.*, p. 408.

[192]Pollard, p. 375.

[193]E.g., Pulke, *Defence*, p. 163.

beauty, though even here it is hard to distinguish the tribute paid to style from that paid to content. The characterization may be only a bit of vague comparison like that in the preface to the Authorized Version, "Hebrew the ancientest, ... Greek the most copious, ... Latin the finest,"[194] or the reference in the preface to the Rhemish New Testament to the Vulgate as the translation "of greatest majesty."[195] The prefaces to the Geneva New Testament and the Geneva Bible combine fairly definite linguistic comment with less obvious references to style: "And because the Hebrew and Greek phrases, which are hard to render in other tongues, and also short, should not be so hard, I have sometimes interpreted them without any whit diminishing the *grace* of the sense, as our language doth use them";[196] "Now as we have chiefly observed the sense, and labored always to restore it to all integrity, so have we most reverently kept the propriety of the words, considering that the Apostles who spoke and wrote to the Gentiles in the Greek tongue, rather constrained them to the lively phrase of the Hebrew, than enterprised far by mollifying their language to speak as the Gentiles did. And for this and other causes we have in many places reserved the Hebrew phrases, notwithstanding that they may seem somewhat hard in their ears that are not well practised and also *delight in the sweet sounding phrases* of the holy Scriptures."[197] On the other hand the Rhemish translators defend the retention of these Hebrew phrases on the ground of stylistic beauty: "There is a certain majesty and more signification in these speeches, and therefore both Greek and Latin keep them, although it is no more the Greek or Latin phrase, than it is the English."[198] Of peculiar interest is Tyndale's estimate of the relative possibilities of Hebrew,

---

[194]Pollard, p. 349.

[195]*Ibid.*, p. 303.

[196]*Ibid.*, p. 277.

[197]Pollard, p. 281.

[198]*Ibid.*, p. 309.

Greek, Latin, and English. Of the Bible he writes: "They will say it cannot be translated into our tongue, it is so rude. It is not so rude as they are false liars. For the Greek tongue agreeth more with the English than with the Latin. And the properties of the Hebrew tongue agreeth a thousand times more with the English than with the Latin. The manner of speaking is both one; so that in a thousand places thou needest not but to translate it into the English word for word; when thou must seek a compass in the Latin, and yet shalt have much work to translate it well-favoredly, so that it have the same grace and sweetness, sense and pure understanding with it in the Latin, and as it hath in the Hebrew."[199] The implication that the English version might possess the "grace and sweetness" of the Hebrew original suggests that Tyndale was not entirely unconscious of the charm which his own work possessed, and which it was to transmit to later renderings.

The questions most definitely discussed by those concerned in the translation of the Bible were questions of vocabulary. Primarily most of these discussions centered around points of doctrine and were concerned as largely with the meaning of the word in the original as with its connotation in English. Yet though not in their first intention linguistic, these discussions of necessity had their bearing on the general problems debated by rhetoricians of the day and occasionally resulted in definite comment on English usage, as when, for example. More says: "And in our English tongue this word senior signifieth nothing at all, but is a French word used in English more than half in mockage, when one will call another my lord in scorn." With the exception of Sir John Cheke few of the translators say anything which can be construed as advocacy of the employment of native English words. Of Cheke's attitude there can, of course, be no doubt. His theory is thus described by Strype: "And moreover, in writing any discourse, he would allow no words, but such as were pure English, or of Saxon

---

[199]Preface to *The Obedience of a Christian Man, Doctrinal Treatises*, pp. 148-9.

original; suffering no adoption of any foreign word into the English speech, which he thought was copious enough of itself, without borrowing words of other countries. Thus in his own translations into English, he would not use any but pure English phrase and expression, which indeed made his style here and there a little affected and hard: and forced him to use sometimes odd and uncouth words."[200] His Biblical translation was a conscious attempt at carrying out these ideas. "Upon this account," writes Strype, "Cheke seemed to dislike the English translation of the Bible, because in it there were so many foreign words. Which made him once attempt a new translation of the New Testament, and he completed the gospel of St. Matthew. And made an entrance into St. Mark; wherein all along he labored to use only true Anglo-Saxon words."[201] Since Cheke's translation remained in manuscript till long after the Elizabethan period, its influence was probably not far-reaching, but his uncompromising views must have had their effect on his contemporaries. Taverner's Bible, a less extreme example of the same tendency, seemingly had no influence on later renderings.[202]

Regarding the value of synonyms there is considerable comment, the prevailing tendency of which is not favorable to unnecessary discrimination between pairs of words. This seems to be the attitude of Coverdale in two somewhat confused passages in which he attempts to consider at the same time the signification of the original word, the practice of other translators, and the facts of English usage. Defending diversities of

---

[200]*Life of Cheke*, p. 212.

[201]*Ibid.*, p. 212.

[202]An interesting comment of later date than the Authorized Version is found in the preface to William L'Isle's *Divers Ancient Monuments of the Saxon Tongue*, published in 1638. L'Isle writes: "These monuments of reverend antiquity, I mean the Saxon Bibles, to him that understandingly reads and well considers the time wherein they were written, will in many places convince of affected obscurity some late translations." After criticizing the inkhorn terms of the Rhemish translators, he says, "The Saxon hath words for Trinity, Unity, and all such foreign words as we are now fain to use, because we have forgot better of our own." (In J. L. Moore, *Tudor-Stuart Views on the Growth, Status, and Destiny of the English Language*.)

translations, he says, "For that one interpreteth something obscurely in one place, the same translateth another, or else he
himself, more manifestly by a more plain vocable of the same
meaning in another place."[203] As illustrations Coverdale mentions scribe and lawyer; elders, and father and mother; repentance, penance, and amendment; and continues: "And in this
manner have I used in my translation, calling at in one place
penance that in another place I call repentance; and that not
only because the interpreters have done so before me, but that
the adversaries of the truth may see, how that we abhor not
this word penance as they untruly report of us, no more than
the interpreters of Latin abhor poenitare, when they read
rescipiscere." In the preface to the Latin-English Testament of
1535 he says: "And though I seem to be all too scrupulous calling it in one place penance, that in another I call repentance:
and gelded that another calleth chaste, this methinks ought
not to offend the saying that the holy ghost (I trust) is the author of both our doings... and therefore I heartily require thee
think no more harm in me for calling it in one place penance
that in another I call repentance, than I think harm in him that
calleth it chaste, which by the nature of this word *Eunuchus* I
call gelded... And for my part I ensure thee I am indifferent to
call it as well with one term as with the other, so long as I
know that it is no prejudice nor injury to the meaning of the
holy ghost."[204] Fulke in his answer to Gregory Martin shows
the same tendency to ignore differences in meaning. Martin
says: "Note also that they put the word 'just,' when faith is
joined withal, as Rom. i, 'the just shall live by faith,' to signify
that justification is by faith. But if works be joined withal and
keeping the commandments, as in the place alleged, Luke i,
there they say 'righteous' to suppose justification by works."
Fulke rephes: "This is a marvellous difference, never heard of
(I think) in the English tongue before, between 'just' and
'righteous,' 'justice' and 'righteousness.' I am sure there is

---

[203] *Prologue* to Bible of 1535.

[204] Pollard, p. 212.

none of our translators, no, nor any professor of justification by faith only, that esteemeth it the worth of one hair, whether you say in any place of scripture 'just' or 'righteous,' 'justice' or 'righteousness'; and therefore freely have they used sometimes the one word, sometimes the other. ... Certain it is that no Englishman knoweth the difference between 'just' and 'righteous,' 'unjust' and 'unrighteous,' saving that 'righteousness' and 'righteous' are the more familiar English words."[205] Martin and Fulke differ in the same way over the use of the words "deeds" and "works." The question whether the same English word should always be used to represent the same word in the original was frequently a matter of discussion. It was probably in the mind of the Archbishop of Ely when he wrote to Archbishop Parker, "And if ye translate bonitas or misericordiam, to use it likewise in all places of the Psalms."[206] The surprising amount of space devoted by the preface to the version of 1611 to explaining the usage followed by the translators gives some idea of the importance attaching to the matter. "We have not tied ourselves," they say, "to an uniformity of phrasing, or to an identity of words, as some peradventure would wish that we had done, because they observe, that some learned men somewhere, have been as exact as they could that way. Truly, that we might not vary from the sense of that which we had translated before, if the word signified the same in both places (for there be some words that be not of the same sense everywhere) we were especially careful, and made a conscience, according to our duty. But that we should express the same notion in the same particular word; as for example, if we translate the *Hebrew* or *Greek* word once by *Purpose*, never to call it *Intent*; if one where *Journeying*, never *Travelling*; if one where *Think*, never *Suppose*; if one where *Pain*, never *Ache*; if one where *Joy*, never *Gladness*, etc. Thus to mince the matter, we thought to savor more of curiosity than wisdom. ... For is the kingdom of God become words or sylla-

---

[205]Fulke, pp. 337-8.

[206]Pollard, p. 291.

bles? why should we be in bondage to them if we may be free, use one precisely when we may use another no less fit, as commodiously?"[207]

It was seldom, however, that the translator felt free to interchange words indiscriminately. Of his treatment of the original Purvey writes: "But in translating of words equivocal, that is, that hath many significations under one letter, may lightly be peril, for Austin saith in the 2nd. book of Christian Teaching, that if equivocal words be not translated into the sense, either understanding, of the author, it is error; as in that place of the Psalm, *the feet of them be swift to shed out blood*, the Greek word is equivocal to *sharp* and *swift*, and he that translated *sharp feet* erred, and a book that hath *sharp feet* is false, and must be amended; as that sentence *unkind young trees shall not give deep roots* oweth to be thus, *the plantings of adultery shall not give deep roots.* ... Therefore a translator hath great need to study well the sentence, both before and after, and look that such equivocal words accord with the sentence."[208] Consideration of the connotation of English words is required of the translators of the Bishops' Bible. "Item that all such words as soundeth in the Old Testament to any offence of lightness or obscenity be expressed with more convenient terms and phrases."[209] Generally, however, it was the theological connotation of words that was at issue, especially the question whether words were to be taken in their ecclesiastical or their profane sense, that is, whether certain words which through long association with the church had come to have a peculiar technical meaning should be represented in English by such words as the church habitually employed, generally words similar in form to the Latin. The question was a large one, and affected other languages than English. Foxe, for example, has difficulty in turning into Latin the controversy between Arch-

---

[207] *Ibid.*, p. 374.

[208] *Prologue*, Chapter 15.

[209] Pollard, p. 298.

bishop Cranmer and Gardiner, Bishop of Winchester. "The English style also stuck with him; which having so many ecclesiastical phrases and manners of speech, no good Latin expressions could be found to answer them."[210] In England trouble arose with the appearance of Tyndale's New Testament. More accused him of mistranslating "three words of great weight,"[211] priests, church, and charity, for which he had substituted *seniors, congregation,* and *love.* Robert Ridley, chaplain to the Bishop of London, wrote of Tyndale's version: "By this translation we shall lose all these Christian words, penance, charity, confession, grace, priest, church, which he always calleth a congregation.—Idolatria calleth he worshipping of images."[212] Much longer is the list of words presented to Convocation some years later by the Bishop of Winchester "which he desired for their germane and native meaning and for the majesty of their matter might be retained as far as possible in their own nature or be turned into English speech as closely as possible."[213] It goes so far as to include words like Pontifex, Ancilla, Lites, Egenus, Zizania. This theory was largely put into practice by the translators of the Rhemish New Testament, who say, "We are very precise and religious in following our copy, the old vulgar approved Latin: not only in sense, which we hope we always do, but sometimes in the very words also and phrases,"[214] and give as illustrations of their usage the retention of Corbana, Parasceve, Pasche, Azymes, and similar words. Between the two extreme positions represented by Tyndale on the one hand and the Rhemish translators on the other, is the attitude of Grindal, who thus advises Foxe in the case previously mentioned: "In all these matters, as also in most others, it will be safe to hold a middle course. My judgment is the same with regard to style. For neither is

---

[210]Strype, *Life of Grindal*, Oxford, 1821, p. 19.

[211]Pollard, p. 127.

[212]*Ibid.*, p. 124.

[213]Pollard, p. 274.

[214]*Ibid.*, p. 305.

the ecclesiastical style to be fastidiously neglected, as it is by some, especially when the heads of controversies cannot sometimes be perspicuously explained without it, nor, on the other hand, is it to be so superstitiously followed as to prevent us sometimes from sprinkling it with the ornaments of language."[215] The Authorized Version, following its custom, approves the middle course: "We have on the one side avoided the scrupulosity of the Puritans, who leave the old Ecclesiastical words, and betake themselves to other, as when they put *washing* for *Baptism,* and *Congregation* instead of *Church*: as also on the other side we have shunned the obscurity of the Papists, in their *Azimes, Tunike, Rational, Holocausts, Praepuce, Pasche,* and a number of such like."[216]

In the interval between Tyndale's translation and the appearance of the Authorized Version the two parties shifted their ground rather amusingly. More accuses Tyndale of taking liberties with the prevailing English usage, especially when he substitutes congregation for church, and insists that the people understand by church what they ought to understand. "This is true," he says, "of the usual signification of these words themselves in the English tongue, by the common custom of us English people, that either now do use these words in owe language, or that have used before our days. And I say that this common custom and usage of speech is the only thing by which we know the right and proper signification of any word, in so much that if a word were taken out of Latin, French, or Spanish, and were for lack of understanding of the tongue from whence it came, used for another thing in English than it was in the former tongue: then signifieth it in England none other thing than as we use it and understand thereby, whatsoever it signify anywhere else. Then say I now that in England this word congregation did never signify the number of Christian people with a connotation or consideration of

---

[215]Translated in *Remains of Archbishop Grindal*, Parker Society, 1843, p. 234.

[216]Pollard, pp. 375-6.

their faith or Christendom, no more than this word assemble, which hath been taken out of the French, and now is by custom become English, as congregation is out of the Latin."[217] Later he returns to the charge with the words, "And then must he with his translation make us an English vocabulary too."[218] In the later period, however, the positions are reversed. The conservative party, represented by the Rhemish translators, admit that they are employing unfamiliar words, but say that it is a question of faithfulness to originals, and that the new words "will easily grow to be current and familiar,"[219] a contention not without basis when one considers how much acceptance or rejection by the English Bible could affect the status of a word. Moreover the introduction of new words into the Scriptures had its parallel in the efforts being made elsewhere to enrich the language. The Rhemish preface, published in 1582, almost contemporaneously with Lyly's *Euphues* and Sidney's *Arcadia*, justifies its practice thus: "And why should we be squamish at new words or phrases in the Scripture, which are necessary: when we do easily admit and follow new words coined in court and in courtly or other secular writings?"[220]

The points at issue received their most thorough consideration in the controversy between Gregory Martin and William Fulke. Martin, one of the translators of the Rhemish Testament, published, in 1582, *A Discovery of the Manifold Corruptions of the Holy Scriptures by the Heretics of our Days*, a book in which apparently he attacked all the Protestant translations with which he was familiar, including Beza's Latin Testament and even attempting to involve the English translators in the same condemnation with Castalio. Fulke, in his *Defence of the Sincere and True Translation of the Holy Scriptures*, reprinted

---

[217]More, *Confutation of Tyndale, Works*, p. 417.

[218]*Ibid.*, p. 427.

[219]Pollard, p. 307.

[220]Pollard, p. 291.

Martin's *Discovery* and replied to it section by section. Both discussions are fragmentary and inconsecutive, but there emerges from them at intervals a clear statement of principles. Fundamentally the positions of the two men are very different. Martin is not concerned with questions of abstract scholarship, but with matters of religious belief. "But because these places concern no controversy," he says, "I say no more."[221] He does not hesitate to place the authority of the Fathers before the results of contemporary scholarship. "For were not he a wise man, that would prefer one Master Humfrey, Master Fulke, Master Whitakers, or some of us poor men, because we have a little smack of the three tongues, before St. Chrysostom, St. Basil, St. Augustine, St. Gregory, or St. Thomas, that understood well none but one?"[222] Since his field is thus narrowed, he finds it easy to lay down definite rules for translation. Fulke, on the other hand, believes that translation may be dissociated from matters of belief. "If the translator's purpose were evil, yet so long as the words and sense of the original tongue will bear him, he cannot justly be called a false and heretical translator, albeit he have a false and heretical meaning."[223] He is not willing to accept unsupported authority, even that of the leaders of his own party. "If Luther misliked the Tigurine translation," he says in another attack on the Rhemish version, "it is not sufficient to discredit it, seeing truth, and not the opinion or authority of men is to be followed in such matters,"[224] and again, in the *Defence*, "The Geneva bibles do not profess to translate out of Beza's Latin, but out of the Hebrew and Greek; and if they agree not always with Beza, what is that to the purpose, if they agree with the truth of the original text?"[225] Throughout the *Defence* he is on

---

[221]*Defence*, p. 42.

[222]*Ibid.*, p 507.

[223]*Defence*, p. 210.

[224]*Confutation of the Rhemish Testament*, New York, 1834, p. 21.

[225]*Defence*, p. 118.

his guard against Martin's attempts to drive him into unqualified acceptance of any set formula of translation.

The crux of the controversy was the treatment of ecclesiastical words. Martin accuses the English translators of interpreting such words in their "etymological" sense, and consulting profane writers. Homer, Pliny, Tully, Virgil,[226] for their meaning, instead of observing the ecclesiastical use, which he calls "the usual taking thereof in all vulgar speech and writing."[227] Fulke admits part of Martin's claim: "We have also answered before that words must not always be translated according to their original and general signification, but according to such signification as by use they are appropried to be taken. We agree also, that words taken by custom of speech into an ecclesiastical meaning are not to be altered into a strange or profane signification."[228] But ecclesiastical authority is not always a safe guide. "How the fathers of the church have used words, it is no rule for translators of the scriptures to follow; who oftentimes used words as the people did take them, and not as they signified in the apostles' time."[229] In difficult cases there is a peculiar advantage in consulting profane writers, "who used the words most indifferently in respect of our controversies of which they were altogether ignorant."[230] Fulke refuses to be reduced to accept entirely either the "common" or the "etymological" interpretation. "A translator that hath regard to interpret for the ignorant people's instruction, may sometimes depart from the etymology or common signification or precise turning of word for word, and that for divers causes."[231] To one principle, however, he will commit himself: the translator must observe common English usage. "We are not lords of the

---

[226] *Ibid.*, p. 160.

[227] *Ibid.*, p. 217.

[228] *Defence*, p. 217.

[229] *Ibid.*, p. 162.

[230] *Ibid.*, p. 161.

[231] *Ibid.*, p. 58.

common speech of men," he writes, "for if we were, we would teach them to use their terms more properly; but seeing we cannot change the use of speech, we follow Aristotle's counsel, which is to speak and use words as the common people useth."[232] Consequently ecclesiastical must always give way to popular usage. "Our meaning is not, that if any Greek terms, or words of any other language, have of long time been usurped in our English language, the true meaning of which is unknown at this day to the common people, but that the same terms may be either in translation or exposition set out plainly, to inform the simplicity of the ignorant, by such words as of them are better understood. Also when those terms are abused by custom of speech, to signify some other thing than they were first appointed for, or else to be taken ambiguously for divers things, we ought not to be superstitious in these cases, but to avoid misunderstanding we may use words according to their original signification, as they were taken in such time as they were written by the instruments of the Holy Ghost."[233]

Fulke's support of the claims of the English language is not confined to general statements. Acquaintance with other languages has given him a definite conception of the properties of his own, even in matters of detail. He resents the importation of foreign idiom. "If you ask for the readiest and most proper English of these words, I must answer you, 'an image, a worshipper of images, and worshipping of images,' as we have sometimes translated. The other that you would have, 'idol, idolater, and idolatry,' be rather Greekish than English words; which though they be used by many Englishmen, yet are they not understood of all as the other be."[234] "You… avoid the names of elders, calling them ancients, and the wise men sages, as though you had rather speak French than English, as

---

[232]*Ibid.*, p. 267.

[233]*Defence*, p. 217.

[234]*Ibid.*, p. 179.

we do; like as you translate *confide*, 'have a good heart,' after the French phrase, rather than you would say as we do, 'be of good comfort.'"[235] Though he admits that English as compared with older languages is defective in vocabulary, he insists that this cannot be remedied by unwarranted coinage of words. "That we have no greater change of words to answer so many of the Hebrew tongue, it is of the riches of that tongue, and the poverty of our mother language, which hath but two words, image and idol, and both of them borrowed of the Latin and Greek: as for other words equivalent, we know not any, and we are loth to make any new words of that signification, except the multitude of Hebrew words of the same sense coming together do sometimes perhaps seem to require it. Therefore as the Greek hath fewer words to express this thing than the Hebrew, so hath the Latin fewer than the Greek, and the English fewest of all, as will appear if you would undertake to give us English words for the thirteen Hebrew words: except you would coin such ridiculous inkhorn terms, as you do in the New Testament, Azymes, prepuce, neophyte, sandale, parasceve, and such like."[236] "When you say 'evangelized,' you do not translate, but feign a new word, which is not understood of mere English ears."[237]

Fulke describes himself as never having been "of counsel with any that translated the scriptures into English,"[238] but his works were regarded with respect, and probably had considerable influence on the version of 1611.[239] Ironically enough, they did much to familiarize the revisers with the Rhemish version and its merits. On the other hand, Fulke's own views had a distinct value. Though on some points he is narrowly conservative, and though some of the words which he con-

---

[235] *Ibid.*, p. 90.

[236] *Defence*, p. 206.

[237] *Ibid.*, p. 549.

[238] *Ibid.*, p. 89.

[239] Pollard, *Introduction*, p. 37.

demns have established themselves in the language nevertheless most of his ideas regarding linguistic usage are remark-
ably sound, and, like those of More, commend themselves to
modern opinion.

Between the translators of the Bible and the translators of
other works there were few points of contact. Though similar
problems confronted both groups, they presented themselves
in different guises. The question of increasing the vocabulary,
for example, is in the case of biblical translation so complicated by the theological connotation of words as to require a
treatment peculiar to itself. Translators of the Bible were
scarcely ever translators of secular works and vice versa. The
chief link between the two kinds of translation is supplied by
the metrical versions of the Psalms. Such verse translations
were counted of sufficient importance to engage the efforts of
men like Parker and Coverdale, influential in the main course
of Bible translation. Men like Thomas Norton, the translator of
Calvin's *Institutes*, Richard Stanyhurst, the translator of *Virgil*,
and others of greater literary fame, Wyatt, Surrey, Sidney, Mil-
ton, Bacon, experimented, as time went on, with these metrical
renderings. The list even includes the name of King James.[240]

At first there was some idea of creating for such songs a vogue
in England like that which the similar productions of Marot
had enjoyed at the French court. Translators felt free to choose
what George Wither calls "easy and passionate Psalms," and,
if they desired, create "elegant-seeming paraphrases…
trimmed… up with rhetorical illustrations (suitable to their
fancies, and the changeable garb of affected language)."[241] The
expectations of courtly approbation were, however, largely
disappointed, but the metrical Psalms came, in time, to have a
wider and more democratic employment. Complete versions
of the Psalms in verse came to be regarded as a suitable ac-

---

[240]See Holland, *The Psalmists of Britain*, London, 1843, for a detailed account of
such translations.

[241]Preface to *The Psalms of David translated into lyric verse*, 1632, reprinted by the
Spenser Society, 1881.

companiment to the Bible, until in the Scottish General Assembly of 1601 the proposition for a new translation of the Bible was accompanied by a parallel proposition for a correction of the Psalms in metre.[242]

Besides this general realization of the practical usefulness of these versions in divine service, there was in some quarters an appreciation of the peculiar literary quality of the Psalms which tended to express itself in new attempts at translation. Arthur Golding, though not himself the author of a metrical version, makes the following comment: "For whereas the other parts of holy writ (whether they be historical, moral, judicial, ceremonial, or prophetical) do commonly set down their treatises in open and plain declaration: this part consisting of them all, wrappeth up things in types and figures, describing them under borrowed personages, and oftentimes winding in matters of prevention, speaking of things to come as if they were past or present, and of things past as if they were in doing, and every man is made a betrayer of the secrets of his own heart. And forasmuch as it consisteth chiefly of prayer and thanksgiving, or (which comprehendeth them both) of invocation, which is a communication with God, and requireth rather an earnest and devout lifting up of the mind than a loud or curious utterance of the voice: there be many imperfect sentences, many broken speeches, and many displaced words: according as the party that prayed, was either prevented with the swiftness of his thoughts, or interrupted with vehemency of joy or grief, or forced to surcease through infirmity, that he might recover more strength and cheerfulness by interminding God's former promises and benefits."[243] George Wither finds that the style of the Psalms demands a verse translation. "The language of the Muses," he declares, "in which the Psalms were originally written, is not so properly expressed in the prose dialect as in verse." "I have used

---

[242]Holland, p. 251.

[243]*Epistle Dedicatory*, to *The Psalms with M. John Calvin's Commentaries*, 1571.

some variety of verse," he explains, "because prayers, praises, lamentations, triumphs, and subjects which are pastoral, heroical, elegiacal, and mixed (all which are found in the Psalms) are not properly expressed in one sort of measure."[244]

Besides such perception of the general poetic quality of the Psalms as is found in Wither's comment, there was some realization that metrical elements were present in various books of Scripture. Jerome, in his *Preface to Job*, had called attention to this,[245] but the regular translators, whose references to Jerome, though frequent, are somewhat vague, apparently made nothing of the suggestion. Elsewhere, however, there was an attempt to justify the inclusion of translations of the Psalms among other metrical experiments. Googe, defending the having of the Psalms in metre, declares that Isaiah, Jeremiah, and other parts of the Bible "were written by the first authors in perfect and pleasant hexameter verses.[246] Stanyhurst[247] and Fraunce[248] both tried putting the Psalms into English hexameters. There was, however, no accurate knowledge of the Hebrew verse system. The preface to the American *Bay Psalm Book*, published in 1640,[249] explains that "The psalms are penned in such verses as are suitable to the poetry of the Hebrew language, and not in the common style of such other books of the Old Testament as are not poetical. ... Then, as all owe English songs (according to the course of our English poetry) do run in metre, so ought David's psalms to be translated into metre, that we may sing the Lord's songs, as in our English tongue so in such verses as are familiar to an English ear, which are commonly metrical." It is not possible to reproduce the Hebrew metres. "As the Lord hath hid from us the

---

[244]*Op. cit.*

[245]See *The Nicene and Post-Nicene Fathers*, ed. Schaff and Wace, New York, 1893, p. 491.

[246]Holland, Note, p. 89.

[247]Published at the end of his *Virgil*.

[248]In *The Countess of Pembroke's Emanuell*, 1591.

[249]Reprinted, New York, 1903.

Hebrew tunes, lest we should think ourselves bound to imitate them; so also the course and frame (for the most part) of their Hebrew poetry, that we might not think ourselves bound to imitate that, but that every nation without scruple might follow as the grave sort of tunes of their own country, so the graver sort of verses of their own country's poetry." This had already become the common solution of the difficulty, so that even Wither keeps to the kinds of verse used in the old Psalm books in order that the old tunes may be used.

But though the metrical versions of the Psalms often inclined to doggerel, and though they probably had little, if any, influence on the Authorized Version, they made their own claims to accuracy, and even after the appearance of the King James Bible sometimes demanded attention as improved renderings. George Wither, for example, believes that in using verse he is being more faithful to the Hebrew than are the prose translations. "There is," he says, "a poetical emphasis in many places, which requires such an alteration in the grammatical expression, as will seem to make some difference in the judgment of the common reader; whereas it giveth best life to the author's intention; and makes that perspicuous which was made obscure by those mere grammatical interpreters, who were not acquainted with the proprieties and liberties of this kind of writing." His version is, indeed, "so easy to be understood, that some readers have confessed, it hath been instead of a comment unto them in sundry hard places." His rendering is not based merely on existing English versions; he has "the warrant of best Hebrew grammarians, the authority of the Septuagint, and Chaldean paraphrase, the example of the ancient and of the best modern prose translators, together with the general practice and allowance of all orthodox expositors." Like Wither, other translators went back to original sources and made their verse renderings real exercises in translation rather than mere variations on the accepted English text. From this point of view their work had perhaps some value; and though it seems regrettable that practically nothing of permanent literary importance should have resulted from such repeated experiments, they are interesting at least as affording some connection between the sphere of the regular translators and the literary world outside.

III. The Sixteenth Century

The Elizabethan period presents translations in astonishing number and variety. As the spirit of the Renaissance began to inspire England, translators responded to its stimulus with an enthusiasm denied to later times. It was work that appealed to persons of varying ranks and of varying degrees of learning. In the early part of the century, according to Nash, "every private scholar, William Turner and who not, began to vaunt their smattering of Latin in English impressions."[250] Thomas Nicholls, the goldsmith, translated Thucydides; Queen Elizabeth translated Boethius. The mention of women in this connection suggests how widely the impulse was diffused. Richard Hyrde says of the translation of Erasmus's *Treatise on the Lord's Prayer*, made by Margaret Roper, the daughter of Sir Thomas More, "And as for the translation thereof, I dare be bold to say it, that whoso list and well can confer and examine the translation with the original, he shall not fail to find that she hath showed herself not only erudite and elegant in either tongue, but hath also used such wisdom, such discreet and substantial judgment, in expressing lively the Latin, as a man may peradventure miss in many things translated and turned by them that bear the name of right wise and very well learned men."[251] Nicholas Udall writes to Queen Katherine that there are a number of women in England who know Greek and Latin and are "in the holy scriptures and theology so ripe that they are able aptly, cunningly, and with much grace either to endite or translate into the vulgar tongue for the public instruction and edifying of the unlearned multitude."[252]

---

[250]Gregory Smith, *Elizabethan Critical Essays*, vol. I, p. 313.

[251]*Introduction*, in Foster Watson, *Vives and the Renaissance Education of Women*, 1912.

[252]Letter prefixed to John, in *Paraphrase of Erasmus on the New Testament*, London, 1548.

The greatness of the field was fitted to arouse and sustain the ardor of English translators. In contrast with the number of manuscripts at command in earlier days, the sixteenth century must have seemed endlessly rich in books. Printing was making the Greek and Latin classics newly accessible, and France and Italy, awake before England to the new life, were storing the vernacular with translations and with new creations. Translators might find their tasks difficult enough and they might flag by the way, as Hoby confesses to have done at the end of the third book of *The Courtier*, but plucking up courage, they went on to the end. Hoby declares, with a vigor that suggests Bunyan's Pilgrim, "I whetted my style and settled myself to take in hand the other three books";[253] Edward Hellowes, after the hesitation which he describes in the Dedication to the 1574 edition of Guevara's *Familiar Epistles*, "began to call to mind my God, my Prince, my country, and also your worship," and so adequately upheld, went on with his undertaking; Arthur Golding, with a breath of relief, sees his rendering of Ovid's *Metamorphoses* at last complete.

> Through Ovid's work of turned shapes I have with painful pace
> Passed on, until I had attained the end of all my race.
> And now I have him made so well acquainted with our tongue,
> As that he may in English verse as in his own be sung."[254]

Sometimes the toilsomeness of the journey was lightened by companionship. Now and then, especially in the case of religious works, there was collaboration. Luther's *Commentary on Galatians* was undertaken by "certain godly men," of whom "some began it according to such skill as they had. Others godly affected, not suffering so good a matter in handling to be marred, put to their helping hands for the better framing

---

[253] *Dedication*, 1588.

[254] *To the Reader*, in *Shakespeare's Ovid*, ed. W. H. D. Rouse, 1904.

and furthering of so worthy a work."[255] From Thomas Norton's record of the conditions under which he translated Calvin's *Institution of the Christian Religion*, it is not difficult to feel the atmosphere of sympathy and encouragement in which he worked. "Therefore in the very beginning of the Queen's Majesty's most blessed reign," he writes, "I translated it out of Latin into English, for the commodity of the Church of Christ, at the special request of my dear friends of worthy memory, Reginald Wolfe and Edward Whitchurch, the one Her Majesty's Printer for the Hebrew, Greek, and Latin tongues, the other her Highness' Printer of the books of Common Prayer. I performed my work in the house of my said friend, Edward Whitchurch, a man well known of upright heart and dealing, an ancient zealous Gospeller, as plain and true a friend as ever I knew living, and as desirous to do anything to common good, specially to the advancement of true religion. … In the doing, hereof I did not only trust mine own wit or ability, but examined my whole doing from sentence to sentence throughout the whole book with conference and overlooking of such learned men, as my translation being allowed by their judgment, I did both satisfy mine own conscience that I had done truly, and their approving of it might be a good warrant to the reader that nothing should herein be delivered him but sound, unmingled and uncorrupted doctrine, even in such sort as the author himself had first framed it. All that I wrote, the grave, learned, and virtuous man, M. David Whitehead (whom I name with honorable remembrance) did among others, compare with the Latin, examining every sentence throughout the whole book. Beside all this, I privately required many, and generally all men with whom I ever had any talk of this matter, that if they found anything either not truly translated or not plainly Englished, they would inform me thereof, promising either to satisfy them or to amend it."[256]

---

[255]Bishop of London's preface *To the Reader*, in *A Commentary of Dr. Martin Luther upon the Epistle of St. Paul to the Galatians*, London, 1577.

[256]Preface to *The Institution of the Christian Religion*, London, 1578.

Norton's next sentence, "Since which time I have not been advertised by any man of anything which they would require to be altered" probably expresses the fate of most of the many requests for criticism that accompany translations, but does not essentially modify the impression he conveys of unusually favorable conditions for such work. One remembers that Tyndale originally anticipated with some confidence a residence in the Bishop of London's house while he translated the Bible. Thomas Wilson, again, says of his translation of some of the orations of Demosthenes that "even in these my small travails both Cambridge and Oxford men have given me their learned advice and in some things have set to their helping hand,"[257] and Florio declares that it is owing to the help and encouragement of "two supporters of knowledge and friendship," Theodore Diodati and Dr. Gwinne, that "upheld and armed" he has "passed the pikes."[258]

The translator was also sustained by a conception of the importance of his work, a conception sometimes exaggerated, but becoming, as the century progressed, clearly and truly defined. Between the lines of the dedication which Henry Parker, Lord Morley, prefixes to his translation of Petrarch's *Triumphs*,[259] one reads a pathetic story of an appreciation which can hardly have equaled the hopes of the author. He writes of "one of late days that was groom of the chamber with that renowned and valiant prince of high memory, Francis the French king, whose name I have forgotten, that did translate these triumphs to that said king, which he took so thankfully that he gave to him for his pains an hundred crowns, to him and to his heirs of inheritance to enjoy to that value in land forever, and took such pleasure in it that wheresoever he went, among his precious jewels that book always carried with him for his pastime to look upon, and as much esteemed

---

[257] Preface to *The Three Orations of Demosthenes*, London, 1570.

[258] Dedication of *Montaigne's Essays*, London, 1603.

[259] Reprinted, Roxburghe Club, 1887.

by him as the richest diamond he had." Moved by patriotic emulation, Lord Morley "translated the said book to that most worthy king, our late sovereign lord of perpetual memory, King Henry the Eighth, who as he was a prince above all others most excellent, so took he the work very thankfully, marvelling much that I could do it, and thinking verily I had not done it without help of some other, better knowing in the Italian tongue than I; but when he knew the very truth, that I had translated the work myself, he was more pleased therewith than he was before, and so what his highness did with it is to me unknown."

Hyperbole in estimating the value of the translator's work is not common among Lord Morley's successors, but their very recognition of the secondary importance of translation often resulted in a modest yet dignified insistence on its real value. Richard Eden says that he has labored "not as an author but as a translator, lest I be injurious to any man in ascribing to myself the travail of other."[260] Nicholas Grimald qualifies a translation of Cicero as "my work," and immediately adds, "I call it mine as Plautus and Terence called the comedies theirs which they made out of Greek."[261] Harrington, the translator of *Orlando Furioso*, says of his work: "I had rather men should see and know that I borrow at all than that I steal any, and I would wish to be called rather one of the worst translators than one of the meaner makers, specially since the Earl of Surrey and Sir Thomas Wiat, that are yet called the first refiners of the English tongue, were both translators out of the Italian. Now for those that count it such a contemptible and trifling matter to translate, I will but say to them as M. Bartholomew Clarke, an excellent learned man and a right good translator, said in a manner of pretty challenge, in his Preface (as I remember) upon the Courtier, which book he translated out of Italian into Latin. 'You,' saith he, 'that think it such a toy, lay

[260]Preface to *The Book of Metals*, in Arber, *The First Three English Books on America*, 1885.

[261]Dedication of *Marcus Tullius Cicero's Three Books of Duties*, 1558.

aside my book, and take my author in hand, and try a leaf or such a matter, and compare it with mine.'"[262] Philemon Holland, the "translator general" of his time, writes of his art: "As for myself, since it is neither my hap nor hope to attain to such perfection as to bring forth something of mine own which may quit the pains of a reader, and much less to perform any action that might minister matter to a writer, and yet so far bound unto my native country and the blessed state wherein I have lived, as to render an account of my years passed and studies employed, during this long time of peace and tranquility, wherein (under the most gracious and happy government of a peerless princess, assisted with so prudent, politic, and learned Counsel) all good literature hath had free progress and flourished in no age so much: methought I owed this duty, to leave for my part also (after many others) some small memorial, that might give testimony another day what fruits generally this peaceable age of ours hath produced. Endeavored I have therefore to stand in the third rank, and bestowed those hours which might be spared from the practice of my profession and the necessary cares of life, to satisfy my countrymen now living and to gratify the age ensuing in this kind."[263] To Holland's simple acceptance of his rightful place, it is pleasant to add the lines of the poet Daniel, whose imagination was stirred in true Elizabethan fashion by the larger relations of the translator. Addressing Florio, the interpreter of Montaigne to the English people, he thanks him on behalf of both author and readers for

> ... his studious care
> Who both of him and us doth merit much,
> Having as sumptuously as he is rare
> Placed him in the best lodging of our speech,
> And made him now as free as if born here,
> And as well ours as theirs, who may be proud

---

[262]*A Brief Apology for Poetry*, in Gregory Smith, vol. 2, p. 219.

[263]Preface to *The Natural History of C. Plinius Secundus*, London, 1601.

> To have the franchise of his worth allowed.
> It being the proportion of a happy pen,
> Not to b'invassal'd to one monarchy,
> But dwell with all the better world of men
> Whose spirits are of one community,
> Whom neither Ocean, Deserts, Rocks, nor Sands
> Can keep from th' intertraffic of the mind."[264]

In a less exalted strain come suggestions that the translator's work is valuable enough to deserve some tangible recognition. Thomas Fortescue urges his reader to consider the case of workmen like himself, "assuring thyself that none in any sort do better deserve of their country, that none swink or sweat with like pain and anguish, that none in like sort hazard or adventure their credit, that none desire less stipend or salary for their travail, that none in fine are worse in this age recompensed."[265] Nicholas Udall presents detailed reasons why it is to be desired that "some able, worthy, and meet persons for doing such public benefit to the commonweal as translating of good works and writing of chronicles might by some good provision and means have some condign sustentation in the same."[266] "Besides," he argues, "that such a translator travaileth not to his own private commodity, but to the benefit and public use of his country: besides that the thing is such as must so thoroughly occupy and possess the doer, and must have him so attent to apply that same exercise only, that he may not during that season take in hand any other trade of business whereby to purchase his living: besides that the thing cannot be done without bestowing of long time, great watching, much pains, diligent study, no small charges, as well of meat, drink, books, as also of other necessaries, the labor self is of itself a more painful and more tedious thing than for a man to write or prosecute any argument of his own invention.

---

[264]*Letter to John Florio*, in *Florio's Montaigne*, Tudor Translations.

[265]*To the Reader*, in *The Forest*, London, 1576.

[266]Dedication to Edward VI, in *Paraphrase of Erasmus*.

A man hath his own invention ready at his own pleasure without lets or stops, to make such discourse as his argument requireth: but a translator must... at every other word stay, and suspend both his cogitation and his pen to look upon his author, so that he might in equal time make thrice as much as he can be able to translate."

The belief present in the comment of both Fortescue and Udall that the work of the translator is of peculiar service to the state is expressed in connection with translations of every sort. Richard Taverner declares that he has been incited to put into English part of the *Chiliades* of Erasmus by "the love I bear to the furtherance and adornment of my native country."[267] William Warde translates *The Secrets of Maister Alexis of Piemont* in order that "as well Englishmen as Italians, Frenchmen, or Dutchmen may suck knowledge and profit hereof."[268] John Brende, in the Dedication of his *History of Quintus Curtius*, insists on the importance of historical knowledge, his appreciation of which has made him desire "that we Englishmen might be found as forward in that behalf as other nations, which have brought all worthy histories into their national language."[269] Patriotic emulation of what has been done in other countries is everywhere present as a motive. Occasionally the Englishman shows that he has studied foreign translations for his own guidance. Adlington, in his preface to his rendering of *The Golden Ass* of Apuleius, says that he does not follow the original in certain respects, "for so the French and Spanish translators have not done";[270] Hoby says of his translation of *The Courtier*, "I have endeavored myself to follow the very meaning and words of the author, without being misled by fantasy or leaving out any parcel one or other, whereof I know not how some interpreters of this book into other lan-

---

[267] *Prologue to Proverbs or Adagies with new additions gathered out of the Chiliades of Erasmus by Richard Taverner*, London, 1539.

[268] *Epistle* prefixed to translation, 1568.

[269] Published, Tottell, 1561.

[270] Reprinted, London, 1915.

guages can excuse themselves, and the more they be con-
ferred, the more it will perchance appear."[271] On the whole,
however, the comment confines itself to general statements
like that of Grimald, who in translating Cicero is endeavoring
"to do likewise for my countrymen as Italians, Frenchmen,
Spaniards, Dutchmen, and other foreigners have liberally
done for theirs."[272] In spite of the remarkable output England
lagged behind other countries. Lord Morley complains that
the printing of a merry jest is more profitable than the putting
forth of such excellent works as those of Petrarch, of which
England has "very few or none, which I do lament in my
heart, considering that as well in French as in the Italian (in
the which both tongues I have some little knowledge) there is
no excellent work in the Latin, but that straightway they set it
forth in the vulgar."[273] Morley wrote in the early days of the
movement for translation, but later translators made similar
complaints. Hoby says in the preface to *The Courtier*: "In this
point (I know not by what destiny) Englishmen are most inferior to most of all other nations: for where they set their delight and bend themselves with an honest strife of matching
others to turn into their mother tongue not only the witty writings of other languages but also of all philosophers, and all
sciences both Greek and Latin, our men ween it sufficient to
have a perfect knowledge to no other end but to profit themselves and (as it were) after much pains in breaking up a gap
bestow no less to close it up again." To the end of the century
translation is encouraged or defended on the ground that it is
a public duty. Thomas Danett is urged to translate the *History*
of Philip de Comines by certain gentlemen who think it "a
great dishonor to our native land that so worthy a history being extant in all languages almost in Christendom should be
suppressed in ours";[274] Chapman writes indignantly of

---

[271]*Dedication* in edition of 1588.

[272]*Op. cit.*

[273]*Dedication, op. cit.*

[274]*Dedication*, dated 1596, of *The History of Philip de Comines*, London, 1601.

Homer, "And if Italian, French, and Spanish have not made it dainty, nor thought it any presumption to turn him into their languages, but a fit and honorable labor and (in respect of their country's profit and their prince's credit) almost necessary, what curious, proud, and poor shamefastness should let an English muse to traduce him?"[275]

Besides all this, the translator's conception of his audience encouraged and guided his pen. While translations in general could not pretend to the strength and universality of appeal which belonged to the Bible, nevertheless taken in the mass and judged only by the comment associated with them, they suggest a varied public and a surprising contact with the essential interests of mankind. The appeals on title pages and in prefaces to all kinds of people, from ladies and gentlemen of rank to the common and simple sort, not infrequently resemble the calculated praises of the advertiser, but admitting this, there still remains much that implies a simple confidence in the response of friendly readers. Rightly or wrongly, the translator presupposes for himself in many cases an audience far removed from academic preoccupations. Richard Eden, translating from the Spanish Martin Cortes' *Arte de Navigar*, says, "Now therefore this work of the Art of Navigation being published in our vulgar tongue, you may be assured to have more store of skilful pilots."[276] Golding's translations of Pomponius Mela and Julius Solinus Polyhistor are described as, "Right pleasant and profitable for Gentlemen, Merchants, Mariners, and Travellers."[277] Hellowes, with an excess of rhetoric which takes from his convincingness, presents Guevara's *Familiar Epistles* as teaching "rules for kings to rule, counselors to counsel, prelates to practise, captains to execute, soldiers to perform, the married to follow, the prosperous to prosecute, and the poor in adversity to be comforted, how to write and

---

[275]*Dedication of Achilles"Shield* in Gregory Smith, vol. 2, p. 300.

[276]*Preface* in Arber, *op. cit.*

[277]*Preface*, dated 1584, to translation published 1590.

talk with all men in all matters at large."[278] Holland's honest
simplicity gives greater weight to a similarly sweeping characterization of Pliny's *Natural History* as "not appropriate to the
learned only, but accommodate to the rude peasant of the
country; fitted for the painful artisan in town or city; pertinent
to the bodily health of man, woman, or child; and in one word
suiting with all sorts of people living in a society and commonweal."[279] In the same preface the need for replying to
those who oppose translation leads Holland to insist further
on the practical applicability of his matter. Alternating his
own with his critics' position, he writes: "It is a shame (quoth
one) that *Livy* speaketh English as he doth; Latinists only owe
to be acquainted with him: as who should say the soldier were
to have recourse to the university for military skill and knowledge, or the scholar to put on arms and pitch a camp. What
should Pliny (saith another) be read in English and the mys-
teries couched in his books divulged; as if the husbandman,
the mason, carpenter, goldsmith, lapidary, and engraver, with
other artificers, were bound to seek unto great clerks or lin-
guists for instructions in their several arts." Wilson's translation of Demosthenes, again, undertaken, it has been said, with
a view to rousing a national resistance against Spain, is described on the title page as "most needful to be read in these
dangerous days of all them that love their country's liberty."[280]

Naturally enough, however, especially in the case of translations from the Latin and Greek, the academic interest bulks
largely in the audience, and sometimes makes an unexpected
demand for recognition in the midst of the more practical appeal. Holland's *Pliny*, for example, addresses itself not only to
peasants and artisans but to young students, who "by the light
of the English… shall be able more readily to go away with
the dark phrase and obscure constructions of the Latin."

---

[278]Title page, 1574.

[279]*To the Reader, op. cit.*

[280]London, 1570.

Chapman, refusing to be burdened with a popular audience, begins a preface with the insidious compliment, "I suppose you to be no mere reader, since you intend to read Homer."[281] On the other hand, the academic reader, whether student or critic, is, if one accepts the translator's view, very much on the alert, anxious to confer the English version with the original, either that he may improve his own knowledge of the foreign language or that he may pick faults in the new rendering. Wilson attacks the critics as "drones and no bees, lubbers and no learners," but the fault he finds in these "croaking paddocks and manifest overweeners of themselves" is that they are "out of reason curious judges over the travail and painstaking of others" instead of being themselves producers.[282] Apparently there was little fear of the indifference which is more discouraging than hostile criticism, and though, as is to be expected, it is the hostile criticism that is most often reflected in prefaces, there must have been much kindly comment like that of Webbe, who, after discussing the relations of Phaer's *Virgil* to the Latin, concludes, "There is not one book among the twelve which will not yield you most excellent pleasure in conferring the translation with the copy and marking the gallant grace which our English speech affordeth."[283]

Such encouragements and incentives are enough to awaken the envy of the modern translator. But the sixteenth century had also its peculiar difficulties. The English language was neither so rich in resources nor so carefully standardized as it has become of later times. It was often necessary, indeed, to defend it against the charge that it was not equal to translation. Pettie is driven to reply to those who oppose the use of the vernacular because "they count it barren, they count it barbarous, they count it unworthy to be accounted of."[284] Chap-

---

[281]Preface to *Seven Books of the Iliad of Homer*, in Gregory Smith, vol. 2, p. 293.

[282]*Op. cit.*

[283]Gregory Smith, vol. 1, p. 262.

[284]Preface to *Civile Conversation of Stephen Guazzo*, 1586.

man says in his preface to *Achilles' Shield*: "Some will convey their imperfections under his Greek shield, and from thence bestow bitter arrows against the traduction, affirming their want of admiration grows from the defect of our language, not able to express the copiousness (coppie) and elegancy of the original." Richard Green way, who translated the *Annals* of Tacitus, admits cautiously that his medium is "perchance not so fit to set out a piece drawn with so curious a pencil."[285] One cannot, indeed, help recognizing that as compared with modern English Elizabethan English was weak in resources, limited in vocabulary, and somewhat uncertain in sentence structure. These disadvantages probably account in part for such explanations of the relative difficulty of translation as that of Nicholas Udall in his plea that translators should be suitably recompensed or that of John Brende in his preface to the translation of Quintus Curtius that "in translation a man cannot always use his own vein, but shall be compelled to tread in the author's steps, which is a harder and more difficult thing to do, than to walk his own pace."[286]

Of his difficulties with sentence structure the translator says little, a fact rather surprising to the modern reader, conscious as he is of the awkwardness of the Elizabethan sentence. Now and then, however, he hints at the problems which have arisen in the handling of the Latin period. Udall writes of his translation of Erasmus: "I have in some places been driven to use mine own judgment in rendering the true sense of the book, to speak nothing of a great number of sentences, which by reason of so many members, or parentheses, or digressions as have come in places, are so long that unless they had been somewhat divided, they would have been too hard for an unlearned brain to conceive, much more hard to contain and keep it still."[287] Adlington, the translator of *The Golden Ass* of

---

[285]Dedication of *The End of Nero and Beginning of Galba*, 1598.

[286]*Op. cit.*

[287]*Address to Queen Katherine*, prefixed to Luke.

Apuleius, says, "I have not so exactly passed through the author as to point every sentence exactly as it is in the Latin."[288] A comment of Foxe on his difficulty in translating contemporary English into Latin suggests that he at least was conscious of the weakness of the English sentence as compared with the Latin. Writing to Peter Martyr of his Latin version of the controversy between Cranmer and Gardiner, he says of the latter: "In his periods, for the most part, he is so profuse, that he seems twice to forget himself, rather than to find his end. The whole phrase hath in effect that structure that consisting for the most part of relatives, it refuses almost all the grace of translation."[289]

Though the question of sentence structire was not given prominence, the problem of rectifying deficiencies in vocabulary touched the translator very nearly. The possibility of augmenting the language was a vital issue in the reign of Elizabeth, but it had a peculiar significance where translation was concerned. Here, if anywhere, the need for a large vocabulary was felt, and in translations many new words first made their appearance. Sir Thomas Elyot early made the connection between translation and the movement for increase in vocabulary. In the *Proheme* to *The Knowledge which maketh a wise man* he explains that in *The Governor* he intended "to augment the English tongue, whereby men should... interpret out of Greek, Latin, or any other tongue into English."[290] Later in the century Peele praises the translator Harrington,

> ... well-letter'd and discreet,
> That hath so purely naturalized
> Strange words, and made them all free denizens,[291]

and—to go somewhat outside the period—the fourth edition of Bullokar's *English Expositor*, originally designed to teach

---

[288] *Preface.*

[289] Translated in Strype, *Life of Grindal*, Oxford, 1821, p. 22.

[290] Preface to *The Governor*, ed. Croft.

[291] *Ad Maecenatem Prologus to Order of the Garter*, in *Works*, ed. Dyce, p. 584.

"the interpretation of the hardest words used in our language," is recommended on the ground that those who know no language but the mother tongue, but "are yet studiously desirous to read those learned and elegant treatises which from their native original have been rendered English (of which sort, thanks to the company of painful translators we have not a few) have here a volume fit for their purposes, as carefully designed for their assistance."[292]

Whether, however, the translator should be allowed to add to the vocabulary and what methods he should employ were questions by no means easy of settlement. As in Caxton's time, two possible means of acquiring new words were suggested, naturalization of foreign words and revival of words from older English sources. Against the first of these methods there was a good deal of prejudice. Grimald in his preface to his translation of Cicero's *De Officiis*, protests against the translation that is "uttered with inkhorn terms and not with usual words." Other critics are more specific in their condemnation of non-English words. Puttenham complains that Southern, in translating Ronsard's French rendering of Pindar's hymns and Anacreon's odes, "doth so impudently rob the French poet both of his praise and also of his French terms, that I cannot so much pity him as be angry with him for his injurious dealing, our said maker not being ashamed to use these French words, *freddon, egar, suberbous, filanding, celest, calabrois, thebanois* and a number of others, which have no manner of conformity with our language either by custom or derivation which may make them tolerable."[293] Richard Willes, in his preface to the 1577 edition of Eden's *History of Travel in the West and East Indies*, says that though English literature owes a large debt to Eden, still "many of his English words cannot be excused in my opinion for smelling too much of the Latin."[294] The list ap-

---

[292]Quoted in J. L. Moore, *Tudor-Stuart Views on the Growth, Status, and Destiny of the English Language.*

[293]In Gregory Smith, *Elizabethan Critical Essays*, vol. 2, p. 171.

[294]Quoted in Moore, *op. cit.*

pended is not so remote from the modern English vocabulary as that which Puttenham supplies. Willes cites "*dominators, ponderous, ditionaries, portentous, antiques, despicable, solicitate, obsequious, homicide, imbibed, destructive, prodigious*, with other such like, in the stead of *lords, weighty, subjects, wonderful, ancient, low, careful, dutiful, man-slaughter, drunken, noisome, monstrous*, &c." Yet there were some advocates of the use of foreign words. Florio admits with mock humility that he has employed "some uncouth terms as *entraine, conscientious, endear, tarnish, comport, efface, facilitate, amusing debauching, regret, effort, emotion*, and such like," and continues, "If you like them not, take others most commonly set by them to expound them, since they were set to make such likely French words familiar with our English, which may well bear them,"[295] a contention which modern usage supports. Nicholas Udall pronounces judicially in favor of both methods of enriching the language. "Some there be," he says, "which have a mind to renew terms that are now almost worn clean out of use, which I do not disallow, so it be done with judgment. Some others would ampliate and enrich their native tongue with more vocables, which also I commend, if it be aptly and wittily assayed. So that if any other do innovate and bring up to me a word afore not used or not heard, I would not dispraise it: and that I do attempt to bring it into use, another man should not cavil at."[296] George Pettie also defends the use of inkhorn terms. "Though for my part," he says, "I use those words as little as any, yet I know no reason why I should not use them, for it is indeed the ready way to enrich our tongue and make it copious."[297] On the whole, however, it was safer to advocate the formation of words from Anglo-Saxon sources. Golding says of his translation of Philip of Mornay: "Great care hath been taken by forming and deriving of fit names and terms out of the fountains of our own tongue, though not altogether most usual yet always

---

[295] *To the Reader*, in 1603 edition of *Montaigne's Essays*.

[296] *Address to Queen Katherine*, prefixed to Luke.

[297] *To the Reader* in *Civile Conversation of Stephen Guazzo*, 1586.

conceivable and easy to be understood; rather than by usurping Latin terms, or by borrowing the words of any foreign language, lest the matters, which in some cases are mystical enough of themselves by reason of their own profoundness, might have been made more obscure to the unlearned by setting them down in terms utterly unknown to them."[298] Holland says in the preface to his translation of Livy: "I framed my pen, not to any affected phrase, but to a mean and popular style. Wherein if I have called again into use some old words, let it be attributed to the love of my country's language." Even in this matter of vocabulary, it will be noted, there was something of the stimulus of patriotism, and the possibility of improving his native tongue must have appealed to the translator's creative power. Phaer, indeed, alleges as one of his motives for translating Virgil "defence of my country's language, which I have heard discommended of many, and esteemed of some to be more than barbarous."[299]

Convinced, then, that his undertaking, though difficult, meant much both to the individual and to the state, the translator gladly set about making some part of the great field of foreign literature, ancient and modern, accessible to English readers. Of the technicalities of his art he has a good deal to say. At a time when prefaces and dedications so frequently established personal relations between author and audience, it was natural that the translator also should take his readers into his confidence regarding his aims and methods. His comment, however, is largely incidental. Generally it is applicable only to the work in hand; it does not profess to be a statement, even on a small scale, of what translation in general ought to be. There is no discussion in English corresponding to the small, but comprehensive treatise on *La manière de bien traduire d'une langue en autre* which Étienne Dolet published at Lyons in 1540. This casual quality is evidenced by the peculiar way in which pref-

---

[298] *Preface*, 1587.

[299] *Master Phaer's Conclusion to his Interpretation of the Aeneidos of Virgil*, in edition of 1573.

aces in different editions of the same book appear and disappear for no apparent reason, possibly at the convenience of the printer. It is scarcely fair to interpret as considered, deliberate formulation of principles, utterances so unpremeditated and fragmentary. The theory which accompanies secular translation is much less clear and consecutive than that which accompanies the translation of the Bible. Though in the, latter case the formulation of theories of translation was almost equally incidental, respect for the original, repeated experiment, and constant criticism and discussion united to make certain principles take very definite shape. Secular translation produced nothing so homogeneous. The existence of so many translators, working for the most part independently of each other, resulted in a confused mass of comment whose real value it is difficult to estimate. It is true that the new scholarship with its clearer estimate of literary values and its appreciation of the individual's proprietary rights in his own writings made itself strongly felt in the sphere of secular translation and introduced new standards of accuracy, new definitions of the latitude which might be accorded the translator; but much of the old freedom in handling material, with the accompanying vagueness as to the limits of the translator's function, persisted throughout the time of Elizabeth.

In many cases the standards recognized by sixteenth-century translators were little more exacting than those of the medieval period. With many writers adequate recognition of source was a matter of choice rather than of obligation. The English translator might make suitable attribution of a work to its author and he might undertake to reproduce its substance in its entirety, but he might, on the other hand, fail to acknowledge any indebtedness to a predecessor or he might add or omit material, since he was governed apparently only by the extent of his own powers or by his conception of what would be most pleasing or edifying to his readers. To the theory of his art he gave little serious consideration. He did not attempt to analyse the style of the source which he had chosen. If he praised his author, it was in the conventional language of compliment, which showed no real discrimination and which, one suspects, often disguised mere advertising. His estimate of his own capabilities was only the repetition of the medieval formula, with its profession of inadequacy for the task and its claim to have used simple speech devoid of rhetorical ornament. That it was nothing but a formula was recognized at the time and is good-naturedly pointed out in the words of Harrington: "Certainly if I should confess or rather profess that my verse is unartificial, the style rude, the phrase barbarous, the metre unpleasant, many more would believe it to be so than would imagine that I thought them so."[300]

This medieval quality, less excusable later in the century when the new learning had declared itself, appears with more justification in the comment of the early sixteenth century. Though the translator's field was widening and was becoming more broadly European, the works chosen for translation belonged largely to the types popular in the Middle Ages and the comment attached to them was a repetition of timeworn phrases. Alexander Barclay, who is best known as the author of *The Ship of Fools*, published in 1508, but who also has to his credit several other translations of contemporary moral and allegorical poems from Latin and French and even, in anticipation of the newer era, a version of Sallust's *Jugurthine War*, offers his translations of *The Ship of Fools*[301] and of Mancini's *Mirror of Good Manners* [302] not to the learned, who might judge of their correctness, but to "rude people," who may hope to be benefited morally by perusing them. He has written *The Ship of Fools* in "common and rural terms"; he does not follow the author "word by word"; and though he professes to have reproduced for the most part the "sentence" of the original, he ad-

---

[300]*A Brief Apology for Poetry*, in Gregory Smith, vol. 1, pp. 217-18.

[301]Ed. T. H. Jamieson, Edinburgh, 1874.

[302]Reprinted, Spenser Society, 1885.

mits "sometimes adding, sometimes detracting and taking away such things as seemeth me unnecessary and superfluous."[303] His contemporary. Lord Berners, writes for a more courtly audience, but he professses much the same methods. He introduces his *Arthur of Little Britain*, "not presuming that I have reduced it into fresh, ornate, polished English, for I know myself insufficient in the facundious art of rhetoric, and also I am but a learner, of the language of French: howbeit I trust my simple reason hath led me to the understanding of the true sentence of the matter."[304] Of his translation of Froissart he says, "And in that I have not followed mine author word by word, yet I trust I have ensued the true report of the sentence of the matter."[305] Sir Francis Bryan, under whose direction Berners' translation of *The Golden Book of Marcus Aurelius* was issued in 1535, the year after its author's death, expresses his admiration of the "high and sweet styles"[306] of the versions in other languages which have preceded this English rendering, but similar phrases had been used so often in the characterization of undistinguished writings that this comment hardly suggests the new and peculiar quality of Guevara's style.

As the century advanced, these older, easier standards were maintained especially among translators who chose material similar to that of Barclay and Berners, the popular work of edification, the novella, which took the place of the romance. The purveyors of entertaining narrative, indeed, realized in some degree the minor importance of their work as compared with that of more serious scholars and acted accordingly. The preface to Turbervile's *Tragical Tales* throws some light on the author's idea of the comparative values of translations. He thought of translating Lucan, but Melpomene appeared to warn him against so ambitious an enterprise, and admitting

---

[303] *The Argument.*

[304] Reprinted, London, 1814, *Prologue.*

[305] Ed. E. V. Utterson, London, 1812, *Preface.*

[306] *The Golden Book*, London, 1538, *Conclusion.*

his unfitness for the task, he applied himself instead to this translation "out of sundry Italians."[307] Anthony Munday apologizes for his "simple translation" of *Palmerin d'Oliva* by remarking that "to translate allows little occasion of fine pen work,"[308] a comment which goes far to account for the doubtful quality of his productions in this field.

Even when the translator of pleasant tales ranked his work high, it was generally on the ground that his readers would receive from it profit as well as amusement; he laid no claim to academic correctness. He mentioned or refrained from mentioning his sources at his own discretion. Painter, in inaugurating the vogue of the novella, is exceptionally careful in attributing each story to its author,[309] but Whetstone's *Rock of Regard* contains no hint that it is translated, and *The Petit Palace of Pettie his Pleasure* conveys the impression of original work. "I dare not compare," runs the prefatory *Letter to Gentlewomen Readers* by R. B., "this work with the former Palaces of Pleasure, because comparisons are odious, and because they contain histories, translated out of grave authors and learned writers; and this containeth discourses devised by a green youthful capacity, and repeated in a manner extempore."[310] It was, again, the personal preference of the individual or the extent of his linguistic knowledge that determined whether the translator should employ the original Italian or Spanish versions of some collections or should content himself with an intermediary French rendering. Painter, accurate as he is in describing his sources, confesses that he has often used the French version of Boccaccio, though, or perhaps because, it is less finely written than its original. Thomas Fortescue uses the French version for his translation of *The Forest*, a collection of histories "written in three sundry tongues, in the Spanish first

---

[307]Title page, in Turbervile, *Tragical Tales*, Edinburgh, 1837.

[308]To the Reader, in *Palmerin d'Oliva*, London, 1637.

[309]See Painter, *Palace of Pleasure*, ed. Jacobs, 1890.

[310]*The Petit Palace of Pettie his Pleasure*, ed. Gollancz, 1908.

by Petrus Mexia, and thence done into the Italian, and last into the French by Claudius Gringet, late citizen of Paris."[311] The most regrettable latitude of all, judging by theoretic standards of translation, was the careless freedom which writers of this group were inclined to appropriate. Anthony Munday, to take an extreme case, translating *Palmerin of England* from the French, makes a perfunctory apology in his Epistle Dedicatory for his inaccuracies: "If you find the translation altered, or the true sense in some place of a matter impaired, let this excuse answer in default in that case. A work so large is sufficient to tire so simple a workman in himself. Beside the printer may in some place let an error escape."[312] Fortescue justifies, adequately enough, his omission of various tales by the plea that "the lack of one annoyeth not or maimeth not the other," but incidentally he throws light on the practice of others, less conscientious, who "add or change at their pleasure."

There is perhaps danger of underrating the value of the theory which accompanies translations of this sort. The translators have left comparatively little comment on their methods, and it may be that now and then more satisfactory principles were implicit. Yet even when the translator took his task seriously, his prefatory remarks almost always betrayed that there was something defective in his theory or careless in his execution. Bartholomew Young translates Montemayor's *Diana* from the Spanish after a careful consideration of texts. "Having compared the French copies with the Spanish original," he writes, "I judge the first part to be exquisite, the other two corruptly done, with a confusion of verse into prose, and leaving out in many places divers hard sentences, and some leaves at the end of the third part, wherefore they are but blind guides of any to be imitated."[313] After this, unhappily, in the press of greater affairs he lets the work come from the printer unsupervised

---

[311]*Dedication.*

[312]*Palmerin of England*, ed. Southey, London, 1807.

[313]*Preface to divers learned gentlemen*, in *Diana of George of Montemayor*, London, 1598.

and presumably full of errors, "the copy being very dark and interlined, and I loath to write it out again." Robert Tofte addresses his *Honor's Academy or the Famous Pastoral of the Fair Shepherdess Julietta* "to the courteous and judicious reader and to none other"; he explains that he refuses to write for "the sottish multitude," that monster "who knows not when aught well is or amiss"; and blames "such idle thieves as do purloin from others' mint what's none of their own coin."[314] In spite of this, his preface makes no mention of Nicholas de Montreux, the original author, and if it were not for the phrase on the title page, "done into English," one would not suspect that the book was a translation. The apology of the printer, Thomas Creede, "Some faults no doubt there be, especially in the verses, and to speak truth, how could it be otherwise, when he wrote all this volume (as it were) cursorily and in haste, never having so much leisure as to overlook one leaf after he had scribbled the same," stamps Tofte as perhaps a facile, but certainly not a conscientious workman.

Another fashionable form of literature, the popular religious or didactic work, was governed by standards of translation not unlike those which controlled the fictitious narrative. In the work of Lord Berners the romance had not yet made way for its more sophisticated rival, the novella. His translation from Guevara, however, marked the beginning of a new fashion. While Barclay's *Ship of Fools* and *Mirror of Good Manners* were addressed, like their medieval predecessors, to "lewd" people, with *The Golden Book* began the vogue of a new type of didactic literature, similar in its moral purpose and in its frequent employment of narrative material to the religious works of the Middle Ages, but with new stylistic elements that made their appeal, as did the novella, not to the rustic and unlearned, but to courtly readers. The prefaces to *The Golden Book* and to the translations which succeeded it throw little light on the theory of their authors, but what comment there is points to methods like those employed by the translators of the ro-

---

[314] *To the Reader*, in *Honor's Academy*, London, 1610.

mance and the novella. Though later translators like Hellowes went to the original Spanish, Berners, Bryan, and North employ instead the intermediary French rendering. Praise of Guevara's style becomes a wearisome repetition of conventional phrases, a rhetorical exercise for the English writer rather than a serious attempt to analyze the peculiarities of the Spanish. Exaggeratedly typical is the comment of Hellowes in the 1574 edition of Guevara's *Epistles*, where he repeats with considerable complacency the commendation of the original work which was "contained in my former preface, as followeth. Being furnished so fully with sincere doctrine, so unused eloquence, so high a style, so apt similitudes, so excellent discourses, so convenient examples, so profound sentences, so old antiquities, so ancient histories, such variety of matter, so pleasant recreations, so strange things alleged, and certain parcels of Scripture with such dexterity handled, that it may hardly be discerned, whether shall be greater, either thy pleasure by reading, or profit by following the same."[315]

Guevara himself was perhaps responsible for the failure of his translators to make any formal recognition of responsibility for reproducing his style. His fictitious account of the sources of *The Golden Book* is medieval in tone. He has translated, not word for word, but thought for thought, and for the rudeness of his original he has substituted a more lofty style[316] His English translators reverse the latter process. Hellowes affirms that his translation of the *Epistles* "goeth agreeable unto the Author thereof," but confesses that he wants "both gloss and hue of rare eloquence, used in the polishing of the rest of his works." North later translated from the French Amyot's epoch-making principle: "the office of a fit translator consisteth not only in the faithful expressing of his author's meaning, but also in a certain resembling and shadowing out of the form of his style and manner of his speaking,"[317] but all that he

---

[315] *The Familiar Epistles of Sir Anthony of Guevara*, London, 1574, *To the Reader*.

[316] *Prologue* and *Argument* of Guevara, translated in North, *Dial of Princes*, 1619.
[317] In North, *The Lives of the Noble Grecians and Romans*, 1579.

has to say of his *Dial of Princes* is that he has reduced it into English "according to my small knowledge and tender years."[318] Here again, though the translator may sometimes have tried to adopt newer and more difficult standards, he does not make this explicit in his comment.

Obviously, however, academic standards of accuracy were not likely to make their first appearance in connection with fashionable court literature; one expects to find them associated rather with the translations of the great classical literature, which Renaissance scholars approached with such enthusiasm and respect. One of the first of these, the translation of the *Aeneid* made by the Scotch poet, Gavin Douglas, appeared, like the translations of Barclay and Berners, in the early sixteenth century. Douglas's comment,[319] which shows a good deal of conscious effort at definition of the translator's duties, is an odd mingling of the medieval and the modern. He begins with a eulogy of Virgil couched in the undiscriminating, exaggerated terms of the previous period. Unlike the many medieval redactors of the Troy story, however, he does not assume the historian's liberty of selection and combination from a variety of sources. He regards Virgil as "a per se," and waxes indignant over Caxton's *Eneydos*, whose author represented it as based on a French rendering of the great poet. It is, says Douglas, "no more like than the devil and St. Austin." In proof of this he cites Caxton's treatment of proper names. Douglas claims, reasonably enough, that if he followed his original word for word, the result would be unintelligible, and he appeals to St. Gregory and Horace in support of this contention. All his plea, however, is for freedom rather than accuracy, and one scarcely knows how to interpret his profession of faithfulness:

> And thus I am constrenyt, as neir I may,
> To hald his vers & go nane other way,

---

[318]*Dedication* in edition of 1668.

[319]*Prologue* to Book I, *Aeneid*, reprinted Bannatyne Club.

> Les sum history, subtill word, or the ryme
> Causith me make digressione sum tyme.

Yet whether or not Douglas's "digressions" are permissible, such renderings as he illustrates involve no more latitude than is sanctioned by the schoolboy's Latin Grammar. He is disturbed by the necessity for using more words in English than the Latin has, and he feels it incumbent upon him to explain,

> ... sum tyme of a word I mon mak thre,
> In witness of this term *oppetere.*

English, he says in another place, cannot without the use of additional words reproduce the difference between synonymous terms like *animal* and *homo*; *genus*, *sexus*, and *species*; *objectum* and *subjectum*; *arbor* and *lignum*. Such comment, interesting because definite, is nevertheless no more significant than that which had appeared in the Purvey preface to the Bible more than a hundred years earlier. One is reminded that most of the material which the present-day translator finds in grammars of foreign languages was not yet in existence in any generally accessible form.

Such elementary aids were, however, in process of formulation during the sixteenth century. Mr. Foster Watson quotes from an edition of Mancinus, published as early probably as 1520, the following directions for putting Latin into English: "Whoso will learn to turn Latin into English, let him first take of the easiest Latin, and when he understandeth clearly what the Latin meaneth, let him say the English of every Latin word that way, as the sentence may appear most clearly to his ear, and where the English of the Latin words of the text will not make the sentence fair, let him take the English of those Latin words by whom (which) the Latin words of the text should be expounded and if that (they) will not be enough to make the sentence perfect, let him add more English, and that not only words, but also when need requireth, whole clauses such as will agree best to the sentence."[320] By the new methods of study advocated by men like Cheke and Ascham translation as practiced by students must have become a much more intelligent process, and the literary man who had received such preparatory training must have realized that variations from the original such as had troubled Douglas needed no apology, but might be taken for granted.

Further help was offered to students in the shape of various literal translations from the classics. The translator of Seneca's *Hercules Furens* undertook the work "to conduct by some means to further understanding the unripened scholars of this realm to whom I thought it should be no less thankful for me to interpret some Latin work into this our own tongue than for Erasmus in Latin to expound the Greek."[321] "Neither could I satisfy myself," he continues, "till I had throughout this whole tragedy of Seneca so travailed that I had in English given verse for verse (as far as the English tongue permits) and word for word the Latin, whereby I might both make some trial of myself and as it were teach the little children to go that yet can but creep." Abraham Fleming, translating Virgil's *Georgics* "grammatically," expresses his original "in plain words applied to blunt capacities, considering the expositor's drift to consist in delivering a direct order of construction for the relief of weak grammatists, not in attempting by curious device and disposition to content courtly humanists, whose desire he hath been more willing at this time to suspend, because he would in some exact sort satisfy such as need the supply of his travail."[322] William Bullokar prefaces his translation of Esop's *Fables* with the words: "I have translated out of Latin into English, but not in the best phrase of English, though English be capable of the perfect sense thereof, and might be used in the

---

[320]Foster Watson, *The English Grammar Schools to 1660*, Cambridge, 1908, pp. 405-6.

[321]*Dedication*, in Spearing, *The Elizabethan Translations of Seneca's Tragedies*, Cambridge, 1912.

[322]*To the Reader*, in *The Georgics translated by A. F.*, London, 1589.

best phrase, had not my care been to keep it somewhat nearer the Latin phrase, that the English learner of Latin, reading over these authors in both languages, might the more easily confer them together in their sense, and the better understand the one by the other: and for that respect of easy conference, I have kept the like course in my translation of Tully's *Offices* out of Latin into English to be imprinted shortly also."[323]

Text books like these, valuable and necessary as they were, can scarcely claim a place in the history of literature. Bullokar himself, recognizing this, promises that "if God lend me life and ability to translate any other author into English hereafter, I will bend myself to follow the excellency of English in the best phrase thereof, more than I will bend it to the phrases of the language to be translated." In avoiding the overliteral method, however, the translator of the classics sometimes assumed a regrettable freedom, not only with the words but with the substance of his source. With regard to his translation of the *Aeneid* Phaer represents himself as "Trusting that you, my right worshipful masters and students of universities and such as be teachers of children and readers of this author in Latin, will not be too much offended though every verse answer not to your expectation. For (besides the diversity between a construction and a translation) you know there be many mystical secrets in this writer, which uttered in English would show little pleasure and in my opinion are better to be untouched than to diminish the grace of the rest with tediousness and darkness. I have therefore followed the counsel of Horace, touching the duty of a good interpreter. *Qui quae desperat nitescere posse, relinquit,* by which occasion somewhat I have in places omitted, somewhat altered, and some things I have expounded, and all to the ease of inferior readers, for you that are learned need not to be instructed."[324] Though Jasper Heywood's version of *Hercules Furens* is an example of

---

[323]Preface, reprinted in Plessow, *Fabeldichtung in England*, Berlin, 1906.

[324]*Conclusion*, edition of 1573.

the literal translation for the use of students, most of the other members of the group of young men who in 1581 published their translations of Seneca protest that they have reproduced the meaning, not the words of their author. Alexander Neville, a precocious youth who translated the fifth tragedy in "this sixteenth year of mine age," determined "not to be precise in following the author word for word, but sometimes by addition, sometimes by subtraction, to use the aptest phrases in giving the sense that I could invent."[325] Neville's translation is "oftentimes rudely increased with mine own simple invention";[326] John Studley has changed the first chorus of the *Medea*, "because in it I saw nothing but an heap of profane stories and names of profane idols";[327] Heywood himself, since the existing text of the *Troas* is imperfect, admits having "with addition of mine own pen supplied the want of some things,"[328] and says that he has also replaced the third chorus, because much of it is "heaped number of far and strange countries." Most radical of all is the theory according to which Thomas Drant translated the *Satires* of Horace. That Drant could be faithful even to excess is evident from his preface to *The Wailings of Jeremiah* included in the same volume with his version of Horace. "That thou mightest have this rueful parcel of Scripture pure and sincere, not swerved or altered, I laid it to the touchstone, the native tongue. I weighed it with the Chaldee Targum and the Septuaginta. I desired to jump so nigh with the Hebrew, that it doth erewhile deform the vein of the English, the proprieties of that language and ours being in some speeches so much dissemblable." But with Horace Drant pursues a different course. As a moralist it is justifiable for him to translate Horace because the Latin poet satirizes that

---

[325] *Seneca His Ten Tragedies*, 1581, *Dedication* of Fifth.

[326] *To the Reader.*

[327] *Agamemnom and Medea* from edition of 1656, ed. Spearing, 1913, *Preface* of *Medea*.

[328] *To the Readers*, prefixed to *Troas*, in Spearing, *The Elizabethan Translations of Seneca's Tragedies*.

wickedness which Jeremiah mourned over. Horace's satire, however, is not entirely applicable to conditions in England; "he never saw that with the view of his eye which his pensive translator cannot but overview with the languish of his soul." Moreover Horace's style is capable of improvement, an improvement which Drant is quite ready to provide. "His eloquence is sometimes too sharp, and therefore I have blunted it, and sometimes too dull, and therefore I have whetted it, helping him to ebb and helping him to rise." With his reader Drant is equally high-handed. "I dare not warrant the reader to understand him in all places," he writes, "no more than he did me. Howbeit I have made him more lightsome well nigh by one half (a small accomplishment for one of my continuance) and if thou canst not now in all points perceive him (thou must bear with me) in sooth the default is thine own." After this one is somewhat prepared for Drant's remarkable summary of his methods. "First I have now done as the people of God were commanded to do with their captive women that were handsome and beautiful: I have shaved off his hair and pared off his nails, that is, I have wiped away all his vanity and superfluity of matter. Further, I have for the most part drawn his private carpings of this or that man to a general moral. I have Englished things not according to the vein of the Latin propriety, but of his own vulgar tongue. I have interfered (to remove his obscurity and sometimes to better his matter) much of mine own devising. I have pieced his reason, eked and mended his similitudes, mollified his hardness, prolonged his cortall kind of speeches, changed and much altered his words, but not his sentence, or at least (I dare say) not his purpose."[329] Even the novella does not afford examples of such deliberate justification of undue liberty with source.

Why such a situation existed may be partially explained. The Elizabethan writer was almost as slow as his medieval predecessor to make distinctions between different kinds of litera-

---

[329]*A Medicinable Moral, that is, the two books of Horace his satires Englished according to the prescription of St. Hierome*, London, 1566, *To the Reader.*

ture. Both the novella and the epic might be classed as "histories," and "histories" were valuable because they aided the reader in the actual conduct of life. Arthur Golding tells in the preface to his translation of Justin the story of how Alexander the Great "coming into a school and finding not Homer's works there… gave the master a buffet with his fist: meaning that the knowledge of Histories was a thing necessary to all estates and degrees."[330] It was the content of a work that was most important, and comment like that of Drant makes us realize how persistent was the conception that such content was common property which might be adjusted to the needs of different readers. The lesser freedoms of the translator were probably largely due to the difficulties inherent in a metrical rendering. It is "ryme" that partially accounts for some of Douglas's "digressions." Seneca's *Hercules Furens*, literal as the translation purports to be, is reproduced "verse for verse, as far as the English tongue permits." Thomas Twyne, who completed the work which Phaer began, calls attention to the difficulty "in this kind of translation to enforce their rime to another man's meaning."[331] Edward Hake, it is not unlikely, expresses a common idea when he gives as one of his reasons for employing verse rather than prose "that prose requireth a more exact labor than metre doth."[332] If one is to believe Abraham Fleming, one of the adherents of Gabriel Harvey, matters may be improved by the adoption of classical metres. Fleming has translated Virgil's *Bucolics* and *Georgics* "not in foolish rhyme, the nice observance whereof many times darkeneth, corrupteth, perverteth, and falsifieth both the sense and the signification, but with due proportion and measure."[333]

---

[330]*Preface* to the Earl of Oxford, in *The Abridgment of the Histories of Tragus Pompeius collected and written in the Latin tongue by Justin*, London, 1563.

[331]*To the Gentle Reader*, in Phaer's Virgil, 1583.

[332]*Epistle Dedicatory* to *A Compendious Form of Living*, quoted in Introduction to *News out of Powles Churchyard*, reprinted London, 1872, p. XXX.

[333]*The Bucolics of Virgil together with his Georgics*, London, 1589, *The Argument*.

Seemingly, however, the translators who advocated the employment of the hexameter made little use of the argument that to do so made it possible to reproduce the original more faithfully. Stanyhurst, who says that in his translation of the first four books of the *Aeneid* he is carrying out Ascham's wish that the university students should "apply their wits in beautifying our English language with heroical verses," chooses Virgil as the subject of his experiment for "his peerless style and matchless stuff,"[334] leaving his reader with the impression that the claims of his author were probably subordinate in the translator's mind to his interest in Ascham's theories. Possibly he shared his master's belief that "even the best translation is for mere necessity but an evil imped wing to fly withal, or a heavy stump leg of wood to go withal."[335] In discussion of the style to be employed in the metrical rendering there was the same failure to make explicit the connection between the original and the translation. Many critics accepted the principle that "decorum" of style was essential in the translation of certain kinds of poetry, but they based their demand for this quality on its extrinsic suitability much more than on its presence in the work to be translated. In Turbervile's elaborate comment on the style which he has used in his translation of the *Eclogues* of Mantuan, there is the same baffling vagueness in his references to the quality of the original that is felt in the prefaces of Lydgate and Caxton. "Though I have altered the tongue," he says, "I trust I have not changed the author's meaning or sense in anything, but played the part of a true interpreter, observing that we call Decorum in each respect, as far as the poet's and our mother tongue will give me leave. For as the conference between shepherds is familiar stuff and homely, so have I shaped my style and tempered it with such common and ordinary phrase of speech as countrymen do use in their affairs; alway minding the saying of Horace, whose sentence I have thus Englished:

---

[334]Preface in Gregory Smith, vol. 1, p. 137.

[335]*The Schoolmaster*, in *Works*, London, 1864, vol. 3, p. 226.

To set a manly head upon a horse's neck
And all the limbs with divers plumes of divers hue to
deck,
Or paint a woman's face aloft to open show,
And make the picture end in fish with scaly skin below,
I think (my friends) would cause you laugh and smile
to see
How ill these ill-compacted things and numbers would
agree.

For indeed he that shall translate a shepherd's tale and use the talk and style of an heroical personage, expressing the silly man's meaning with lofty thundering words, in my simple judgment joins (as Horace saith) a horse's neck and a man's head together. For as the one were monstrous to see, so were the other too fond and foolish to read. Wherefore I have (I say) used the common country phrase according to the person of the speakers in every Eclogue, as though indeed the man himself should tell his tale. If there be anything herein that thou shalt happen to mistake, neither blame the learned poet, nor control the clownish shepherd (good reader) but me that presumed rashly to offer so unworthy matter to thy survey."[336] Another phase of "decorum," the necessity for employing a lofty style in dealing with the affairs of great persons, comes in for discussion in connection with translations of Seneca and Virgil. Jasper Heywood makes his excuses in case his translation of the *Troas* has "not kept the royalty of speech meet for a tragedy";[337] Stanyhurst praises Phaer for his "picked and lofty words";[338] but he himself is blamed by Puttenham because his own words lack dignity. "In speaking or writing of a prince's affairs and fortunes," writes Puttenham, "there is a certain decorum, that we may not use the same terms in their business as we might very well do in a meaner person's, the case

---

[336] *To the Reader*, prefixed to translation of *Eclogues* of Mantuan, 1567.

[337] *To the Reader*, in *The Elizabethan Translations of Seneca's Tragedies*.

[338] Stanyhurst's Aeneid, in Arber's Scholar's Library, p. 5.

being all one, such reverence is due to their estates."[339] He instances Stanyhurst's renderings, "Aeneas was fain to *trudge* out of Troy" and "what moved Juno to *tug* so great a captain as Aeneas," and declares that the term *trudge* is "better to be spoken of a beggar, or of a rogue, or of a lackey," and that the word *tug* "spoken in this case is so undecent as none other could have been devised, and took his first original from the cart." A similar objection to the employment of a "plain" style in telling the Troy story was made, it will be remembered, in the early fifteenth century by Wyntoun.

The matter of decorum was to receive further attention in the seventeenth and eighteenth centuries. In general, however, the comment associated with verse translations does not anticipate that of later times and is scarcely more significant than that which accompanies the novella. So long, indeed, as the theory of translation was so largely concerned with the claims of the reader, there was little room for initiative. It was no mark of originality to say that the translation must be profitable or entertaining, clear and easily understood; these rules had already been laid down by generations of translators. The real opportunity for a fresh, individual approach to the problems of translation lay in consideration of the claims of the original author. Renaissance scholarship was bringing a new knowledge of texts and authors and encouraging a new alertness of mind in approaching texts written in foreign languages. It was now possible, while making faithfulness to source obligatory instead of optional, to put the matter on a reasonable basis. The most vigorous and suggestive comment came from a small number of men of scholarly tastes and of active minds, who brought to the subject both learning and enthusiasm, and who were not content with vague, conventional forms of words.

It was prose rather than verse renderings that occupied the attention of these theorists, and in the works which they chose

---

[339] *Ibid.*, *Introduction*, p. xix, quoted from *The Art of English Poesy*.

for translation the intellectual was generally stronger than the artistic appeal. Their translations, however, showed a variety peculiarly characteristic of the English Renaissance. Interest in classical scholarship was nearly always associated with interest in the new religious doctrines, and hence the new theories of translation were attached impartially either to renderings of the classics or to versions of contemporary theological works, valuable on account of the close, careful thinking which they contained, as contrasted with the more superficial charm of writings like those of Guevara. An Elizabethan scholar, indeed, might have hesitated if asked which was the more important, the Greek or Latin classic or the theological treatise. Nash praises Golding indiscriminately "for his industrious toil in Englishing Ovid's *Metamorphoses*, besides many other exquisite editions of divinity turned by him out of the French tongue into our own."[340] Golding himself, translating one of these "exquisite editions of divinity," Calvin's *Sermons on the Book of Job*, insists so strongly on the "substance, importance, and travail"[341] which belong to the work that one is ready to believe that he ranked it higher than any of his other translations. Nor was the contribution from this field to be despised. Though the translation of the Bible was an isolated task which had few relations with other forms of translation, what few affiliations it developed were almost entirely with theological works like those of Erasmus, Melanchthon, Calvin, and to the translation of such writings Biblical standards of accuracy were transferred. On the other hand the translator of Erasmus or Calvin was likely to have other and very different interests, which did much to save him from a narrow pedantry. Nicholas Udall, for example, who had a large share in the translation of Erasmus's *Paraphrase on the New Testament*, also translated parts of Terence and is best known as the author of *Ralph Roister Doister*. Thomas Norton, who translated Calvin's

---

[340]Preface to Greene's *Menaphon*, in Gregory Smith, vol. 1, p. 316.

[341]*Dedication*, dated 1573, in edition of 1584.

Institution of the Christian Religion, has been credited with a share in *Gorboduc.*

It was towards the middle of the century that these translators began to formulate their views, and probably the decades immediately before and after the accession of Elizabeth were more fruitful in theory than any other part of the period. Certain centers of influence may be rather clearly distinguished. In contemporary references to the early part of the century Sir Thomas Elyot and Sir Thomas More are generally coupled together as authorities on translation. Slightly later St. John's College, Cambridge, "that most famous and fortunate nurse of all learning,"[342] exerted through its masters and students a powerful influence. Much of the fame of the college was due to Sir John Cheke, "a man of men," according to Nash, "supernaturally traded in all tongues." Cheke is associated, in one way and another, with an odd variety of translations—Nicholls' translation of a French version of *Thucydides,*[343] Hoby's *Courtier,*[344] Wilson's *Demosthenes*[345]—suggesting something of the range of his sympathies. Though little of his own comment survives, the echoes of his opinions in Ascham's *Schoolmaster* and the preface to Wilson's *Demosthenes* make one suspect that his teaching was possibly the strongest force at work at the time to produce higher standards for translation. As the century progressed Sir William Cecil, in his early days a distinguished student at St. John's and an intimate associate of Cheke's, maintained, in spite of the cares of state, the tradition of his college as the patron of various translators and the recipient of numerous dedications prefixed to their productions. It is from the midcentury translators, however, that the most distinctive comment emanates. United in various combinations, now by religious sympathies, now by a common en-

---

[342]Gregory Smith, vol. 1, p. 313.

[343]Dedicated to Cheke.

[344]See Cheke's Letter in *The Courtier,* Tudor Translations, London, 1900.

[345]See *Epistle* prefixed to translation.

thusiasm for learning, now by the influence of an individual, they form a group fairly homogeneous so far as their theories of translation are concerned, appreciative of academic correctness, but ready to consider also the claims of the reader and the nature of the vernacular.

The earlier translators, Elyot and More, have left small but significant comment on methods. More's expression of theory was elicited by Tyndale's translation of the Bible; of the technical difficulties involved in his own translation of *The Life of Pico della Mirandola* he says nothing. Elyot is one of the first translators to approach his task from a new angle. Translating from Greek to English, he observed, like Tyndale, the differences and correspondences between the two languages. His *Doctrinal of Princes* was translated "to the intent only that I would assay if our English tongue might receive the quick and proper sentences pronounced by the Greeks."[346] The experiment had interesting results. "And in this experience," he continues, "I have found (if I be not much deceived) that the form of speaking, called in Greek and also in English *Phrasis*, much nearer approacheth to that which at this day we use, than the order of the Latin tongue. I mean in the sentences and not in the words."

A peculiarly good exponent of the new vitality which was taking possession of the theory of translation is Nicholas Udall, whose opinions have been already cited in this chapter. The versatility of intellect evinced by the list of his varied interests, dramatic, academic, religious, showed itself also in his views regarding translation. In the various prefaces and dedications which he contributed to the translation of Erasmus's *Paraphrase* he touches on problems of all sorts—stipends for translators, the augmentation of the English vocabulary, sentence structure in translation, the style of Erasmus, the individual quality in the style of every writer—but all these questions he treats lightly and undogmatically. Translation, according to

---

[346]Quoted in *Life* prefixed to *The Governor*, ed. Croft.

Udall, should not conform to iron rules. He is not disturbed by the diversity of methods exhibited in the Paraphrase. "Though every translator," he writes, "follow his own vein in turning the Latin into English, yet doth none willingly swerve or dissent from the mind and sense of his author, albeit some go more near to the words of the author, and some use the liberty of translating at large, not so precisely binding themselves to the strait interpretation of every word and syllable."[347] In his own share of the translation Udall inclines rather to the free than to the literal method. He has not been able "fully to discharge the office of a good translator,"[348] partly because of the ornate quality of Erasmus's style, partly because he wishes to be understood by the unlearned. He does not feel so scrupulous as he would if he were translating the text of Scripture, though even in the latter connection he is guilty of the heretical opinion that "if the translators were not altogether so precise as they are, but had some more regard to expressing of the sense, I think in my judgment they should do better." It will be noted, however, that Udall's advocacy of freedom is an individual reaction, not the repetition of a formula. The preface to his translation of the *Apophthegmes* of Erasmus helps to redress the balance in favor of accuracy. "I have labored," he says, "to discharge the duty of a translator, that is, keeping and following the sense of my book, to interpret and turn the Latin into English, with as much grace of our vulgar tongue as in my slender power and knowledge hath lain."[349] The rest of the preface shows that Udall, in his concern for the quality of the English, did not make "following the sense" an excuse for undue liberties. Writing "with a regard for young scholars and students, who get great value from comparing languages," he is most careful to note such slight changes and omissions as he has made in the text. Explanations and annotations have been printed "in a small letter with some direc-

---

[347] *Address to Queen Katherine* prefixed to *Paraphrase*.

[348] *Address to Katherine* prefixed to Luke.

[349] *To the Reader*, in edition of 1564, literally reprinted Boston, Lincolnshire, 1877.

tory mark," and "any Greek or Latin verse or word, whereof
the pith and grace of the saying dependeth" has been retained,
a sacrifice to scholarship for which he apologizes to the unlearned reader.

Nicholas Grimald, who published his translation of Cicero's
Offices shortly after the accession of Elizabeth, is much more
dogmatic in his rules for translation than is Udall. "Howbeit
look," runs the preface, "what rule the Rhetorician gives in
precept, to be observed of an Orator in telling of his tale: that
it be short, and without idle words: that it be plain, and without dark sense: that it be provable, and without any swerving
from the truth: the same rule should be used in examining and
judging of translation. For if it be not as brief as the very author's text requireth, what so is added to his perfect style shall
appear superfluous, and to serve rather to the making of some
paraphrase or commentary. Thereto if it be uttered with
inkhorn terms, and not with usual words: or if it be phrased
with wrested or far-fetched forms of speech, not fair but
harsh, not easy but hard, not natural but violent it shall seem
to be. Then also, in case it yield not the meaning of the author,
but either following fancy or misled by error forsakes the true
pattern, it cannot be approved for a faithful and sure interpretation, which ought to be taken for the greatest praise of all."[350]
In Grimald's insistence on a brevity equal to that of the original and in his unmodified opposition to innovations in vocabulary, there is something of pedantic narrowness. His criticism
of Cicero is not illuminating and his estimate, in this connection, of his own accomplishment is amusingly complacent. In
Cicero's work "marvellous is the matter, flowing the eloquence, rich the store of stuff, and full artificial the enditing:
but how I," he continues, "have expressed the same, the more
the book be perused, the better it may chance to appear. None
other translation in our tongue have I seen but one, which is of
all men of any learning so well liked that they repute it and
consider it as none: yet if ye list to compare this somewhat

---

[350] *To the Reader*, in *Marcus Tullius Cicero's Three Books of Duties*, 1658.

with that nothing, peradventure this somewhat will serve somewhat the more." Yet in spite of his limitations Grimald has some breadth of outlook. A work like his own, he believes, can help the reader to a greater command of the vernacular. "Here is for him occasion both to whet his wit and also to file his tongue. For although an Englishman hath his mother tongue and can talk apace as he learned of his dame, yet is it one thing to tittle tattle, I wot not how, or to chatter like a jay, and another to bestow his words wisely, orderly, pleasantly, and pithily." The writer knows men who could speak Latin "readily and well-favoredly, who to have done as much in our language and to have handled the same matter, would have been half black." Careful study of this translation will help a man "as well in the English as the Latin, to weigh well properties of words, fashions of phrases, and the ornaments of both."

Another interesting document is the preface entitled *The Translator to the Reader* which appeared in 1578 in the fourth edition of Thomas Norton's translation of Calvin's *Institution of the Christian Religion*. The opinions which it contains took shape some years earlier, for the author expressly states that the translation has not been changed at all from what it was in the first impression, published in 1561, and that the considerations which he now formulates governed him in the beginning. Norton, like Grimald, insists on extreme accuracy in following the original, but he bases his demand on a truth largely ignored by translators up to this time, the essential relationship between thought and style. He makes the following surprisingly penetrative comment on the nature and significance of Calvin's Latin style: "I considered how the author thereof had of long time purposely labored to write the same most exactly, and to pack great plenty of matter in small room of words, yea and those so circumspectly and precisely ordered, to avoid the cavillations of such, as for enmity to the truth therein contained, would gladly seek and abuse all advantages which might be found by any oversight in penning of it, that the sentences were thereby become so full as nothing might well be added without idle superfluity, and again so nighly pared that nothing might be minished without taking away some necessary substance of matter therein expressed. This manner of writing, beside the peculiar terms of arts and figures, and the difficulty of the matters themselves, being throughout interlaced with the schoolmen's controversies, made a great hardness in the author's own book, in that tongue wherein otherwise he is both plentiful and easy, insomuch that it sufficeth not to read him once, unless you can be content to read in vain." Then follows Norton's estimate of the translator's duty in such a case: "I durst not presume to warrant myself to have his meaning without his words. And they that wot well what it is to translate well and faithfully, specially in matters of religion, do know that not only the grammatical construction of words sufficeth, but the very building and order to observe all advantages of vehemence or grace, by placing or accent of words, maketh much to the true setting forth of a writer's mind." Norton, however, did not entirely forget his readers. He approached his task with "great doubtfulness," fully conscious of the dilemma involved. "If I should follow the words, I saw that of necessity the hardness of the translation must needs be greater than was in the tongue wherein it was originally written. If I should leave the course of words, and grant myself liberty after the natural manner of my own tongue, to say that in English which I conceived to be his meaning in Latin, I plainly perceived how hardly I might escape error." In the end he determined "to follow the words so near as the phrase of the English tongue would suffer me." Unhappily Norton, like Grimald and like some of the translators of the Bible, has an exaggerated regard for brevity. He claims that "if the English book were printed in such paper and letter as the Latin is, it should not exceed the Latin in quantity," and that students "shall not find any more English than shall suffice to construe the Latin withal, except in such few places where the great difference of the phrases of the languages enforced me." Yet he believes that his version is not unnecessarily hard to understand, and he urges readers who have found it difficult to "read it ofter, in which doing you shall find (as many have confessed to me that they have found by experience) that those things which at first reading shall displease you for hardness shall be found so easy as so hard matter would suffer, and for the most part more easy than some other phrase which should with greater looseness and smoother sliding away deceive your understanding."

Thomas Wilson, who dedicated his translation of Demosthenes to Sir William Cecil in 1570, links himself with the earlier group of translators by his detailed references to Cheke. Like Norton he is very conscious of the difficulty of translation. "I never found in my life," he writes of this piece of work, "anything so hard for me to do." "Such a hard thing it is," he adds later, "to bring matter out of any one language into another." A vigorous advocate of translation, however, he does not despise his own tongue. "The cunning is no less," he declares, "and the praise as great in my judgment, to translate anything excellently into English, as into any other language," and he hopes that, if his own attempt proves unsuccessful, others will make the trial, "that such an orator as this is might be so framed to speak our tongue as none were able to amend him, and that he might be found to be most like himself." Wilson comes to his task with all the equipment that the period could afford; his preface gives evidence of a critical acquaintance with numerous Latin renderings of his author. From Cheke, however, he has gained something more valuable, the power to feel the vital, permanent quality in the work of Demosthenes. Cheke, he says, "was moved greatly to like Demosthenes above all others, for that he saw him so familiarly applying himself to the sense and understanding of the common people, that he sticked not to say that none ever was more fit to make an Englishman tell his tale praiseworthily in any open hearing either in parliament or in pulpit or otherwise, than this only orator was." Wilson shares this opinion and, representative of the changing standards of Elizabethan scholarship, prefers Demosthenes to Cicero. "Demosthenes used a plain, familiar manner of writing and speaking in all his actions," he says in his *Preface to the Reader*, "applying himself to the people's nature and to their understanding without using of proheme to win credit or devising conclusion to move affections and to purchase favor after he had done his matters... And were it not better and more wisdom to speak plainly and nakedly after the common sort of men in few words, than to overflow with unnecessary and superfluous eloquence as Cicero is thought sometimes to do." "Never did glass so truly represent man's face," he writes later, "as Demosthenes doth show the world to us, and as it was then, so is it now, and will be so still, till the consummation and end of all things shall be." From Cheke Wilson has received also training in methods of translation and especially in the handling of the vernacular. "Master Cheke's judgment was great," he recalls, "in translating out of one tongue into another, and better skill he had in our English speech to judge of the phrases and properties of words and to divide sentences than any one else that I have known. And often he would English his matters out of the Latin or Greek upon the sudden, by looking of the book only, without reading or construing anything at all, an usage right worthy and very profitable for all men, as well for the understanding of the book, as also for the aptness of framing the author's meaning, and bettering thereby their judgment, and therewithal perfecting their tongue and utterance of speech." In speaking of his own methods, however, Wilson's emphasis is on his faithfulness to the original. "But perhaps," he writes, "whereas I have been somewhat curious to follow Demosthenes' natural phrase, it may be thought that I do speak over bare English. Well I had rather follow his vein, the which was to speak simply and plainly to the common people's understanding, than to overflourish with superfluous speech, although I might thereby be counted equal with the best that ever wrote English."

Though now and then the comment of these men is slightly vague or inconsistent, in general they describe their methods clearly and fully. Other translators, expressing themselves with less sureness and adequacy, leave the impression that they have adopted similar standards. Translations, for example, of Calvin's *Commentary on Acts*[351] and Luther's *Commentary on Galatians*[352] are described on their title pages as "faithfully translated" from the Latin. B. R.'s preface to his translation of Herodotus, though its meaning is somewhat obscured by rhetoric, suggests a suitable regard for the original. "Neither of these," he writes of the two books which he has completed, "are braved out in their colors as the use is nowadays, and yet so seemly as either you will love them because they are modest, or not mislike them because they are not impudent, since in refusing idle pearls to make them seem gaudy, they reject not modest apparel to cause them to go comely. The truth is (Gentlemen) in making the new attire, I was fain to go by their old array, cutting out my cloth by another man's measure, being great difference whether we invent a fashion of our own, or imitate a pattern set down by another. Which I speak not to this end, for that myself could have done more eloquently than our author hath in Greek, but that the course of his writing being most sweet in Greek, converted into English loseth a great part of his grace."[353] Outside of the field of theology or of classical prose there were translators who strove for accuracy. Hoby, profiting doubtless by his association with Cheke, endeavored in translating *The Courtier* "to follow the very meaning and words of the author, without being misled by fantasy, or leaving out any parcel one or other."[354] Robert Peterson claims that his version of Della Casa's *Galateo* is "not cunningly but faithfully translated."[355]

---

[351]Translated by Christopher Featherstone, reprinted, Edinburgh, 1844.

[352]London, 1577.

[353]*To the Gentlemen Readers*, in *Herodotus*, translated by B. R., London, 1584.

[354]*Op. cit.*

[355]*Dedication*, in edition of 1576, reprinted, ed. Spingarn, Boston, 1914.

The printer of Carew's translation of Tasso explains: "In that which is done, I have caused the Italian to be printed together with the English, for the delight and benefit of those gentlemen that love that most lively language. And thereby the learned reader shall see how strict a course the translator hath tied himself in the whole work, usurping as little liberty as any whatsoever as ever wrote with any commendations."[356] Even translators who do not profess to be overfaithful display a consciousness of the existence of definite standards of accuracy. Thomas Chaloner, another of the friends of Cheke, translating Erasmus's *Praise of Folly* for "mean men of baser wits and condition," chooses "to be counted a scant true interpreter." "I have not pained myself," he says, "to render word for word, nor proverb for proverb... which may be thought by some cunning translators a deadly sin."[357] To the author of the *Menechmi* the word "translation" has a distinct connotation. The printer of the work has found him "very loath and unwilling to hazard this to the curious view of envious detraction, being (as he tells me) neither so exactly written as it may carry any name of translation, nor such liberty therein used as that he would notoriously differ from the poet's own order."[358] Richard Knolles, whose translation of Bodin's *Six Books of a Commonweal* was published in 1606, employed both the French and the Latin versions of the treatise, and describes himself as on this account "seeking: therein the true sense and meaning of the author, rather than precisely following the strict rules of a nice translator, in observing the very words of the author."[359] The translators of this later time, however, seldom put into words theories so scholarly as those formulated earlier in the period, when, even though the demand for accuracy might sometimes be exaggerated, it was nevertheless the result of

---

[356]*Preface*, in *Godfrey of Bulloigne*, London, 1594, reprinted in Grosart, *Occasional Issues*, 1881.

[357]*To the Reader*, in edition of 1549.

[358]*The Printer to the Reader*, reprinted in *Shakespeare's Library*, 1875.

[359]*To the Reader.*

thoughtful discrimination. There was some reason why a man like Gabriel Harvey, living towards the end of Elizabeth's reign, should look back with regret to the time when England produced men like Cheke and his contemporaries.[360]

One must frequently remind oneself, however, that the absence of expressed theory need not involve the absence of standards. Among translators as among original writers a fondness for analyzing and describing processes did not necessarily accompany literary skill. Much more activity of mind and respect for originals may have existed among verse translators than is evident from their scanty comment. The most famous prose translators have little to say about their methods. Golding, who produced so much both in verse and prose, and who usually wrote prefaces to his translations, scarcely ever discusses technicalities. Now and then, however, he lets fall an incidental remark which suggests very definite ideals. In translating Caesar, for example, though at first he planned merely to complete Brend's translation, he ended by taking the whole work into his own hands, because, as he says, "I was desirous to have the body of the whole story compacted uniform and of one style throughout,"[361] a comment worthy of a much more modern critic. Philemon Holland, again, contributes almost nothing to theory, though his vigorous defense of his art and his appreciation of the stylistic qualities of his originals bear witness to true scholarly enthusiasm. On the whole, however, though the distinctive contribution of the period is the plea of the renaissance scholars that a reasonable faithfulness should be displayed, the comment of the mass of translators shows little grasp of the new principles. When one considers, in addition to their very inadequate expression of theory, the prevailing characteristics of their practice, the balance turns unmistakably in favor of a careless freedom in translation.

---

[360]See *Works*, ed. Grosart, II, 50.

[361]*Dedication*, London, 1590.

Some of the deficiencies in sixteenth-century theory are supplied by Chapman, who applies himself with considerable zest to laying down the principles which in his opinion should govern poetical translations. Producing his versions of Homer in the last years of the sixteenth and early years of the seventeenth century, he forms a link between the two periods. In some respects he anticipates later critics. He attacks both the overstrict and the overloose methods of translation:

> the brake
> That those translators stick in, that affect
> Their word for word traductions (where they lose
> The free grace of their natural dialect,
> And shame their authors with a forced gloss)
> I laugh to see; and yet as much abhor
> More license from the words than may express
> Their full compression, and make clear the author.[362]

It is literalism, however, which bears the brunt of his attack. He is always conscious, "how pedantical and absurd an affectation it is in the interpretation of any author (much more of Homer) to turn him word for word, when (according to Horace and other best lawgivers to translators) it is the part of every knowing and judicial interpreter, not to follow the number and order of words, but the material things themselves, and sentences to weigh diligently, and to clothe and adorn them with words, and such a style and form of oration, as are most apt for the language in which they are converted."[363] Strangely enough, he thinks this literalism the prevailing fault of translators. He hardly dares present his work

> To reading judgments, since so gen'rally,
> Custom hath made ev'n th'ablest agents err
> In these translations; all so much apply
> Their pains and cunnings word for word to render
> Their patient authors, when they may as well

---

[362] *To the Reader*, in *The Iliads of Homer*, Charles Scribner's Sons, p. xvi.
[363] P. XXV.

> Make fish with fowl, camels with whales, engender,
> Or their tongues' speech in other mouths compell.[364]

Chapman, however, believes that it is possible to overcome the difficulties of translation. Although the "sense and elegancy" of Greek and English are of "distinguished natures," he holds that it requires

> Only a judgment to make both consent
> In sense and elocution; and aspire,
> As well to reach the spirit that was spent
> In his example, as with art to pierce
> His grammar, and etymology of words.

This same theory was taken up by numerous seventeenth and eighteenth century translators. Avoiding as it does the two extremes, it easily commended itself to the reason. Unfortunately it was frequently appropriated by critics who were not inclined to labor strenuously with the problems of translation. One misses in much of the later comment the vigorous thinking of the early Renaissance translators. The theory of translation was not yet regarded as "a common work of building" to which each might contribute, and much that was valuable in sixteenth-century comment was lost by forgetfulness and neglect.

---

[364]P. XV.

IV. From Cowley to Pope

Although the ardor of the Elizabethan translator as he approached the vast, almost unbroken field of foreign literature may well awaken the envy of his modern successor, in many respects the period of Dryden and Pope has more claim to be regarded as the Golden Age of the English translator. Patriotic enthusiasm had, it is true, lost something of its earlier fire, but national conditions were in general not unfavorable to translation. Though the seventeenth century, torn by civil discords, was very unlike the period which Holland had lovingly described as "this long time of peace and tranquility, wherein… all good literature hath had free course and flourished,"[365] yet, despite the rise and fall of governments, the stream of translation flowed on almost uninterruptedly. Sandys' *Ovid* is presented by its author, after his visit to America, as "bred in the New World, of the rudeness whereof it cannot but participate; especially having wars and tumults to bring it to light instead of the Muses,"[366] but the more ordinary translation, bred at home in England during the seventeenth century, apparently suffered little from the political strife which surrounded it, while the eighteenth century afforded a "peace and tranquility" even greater than that which had prevailed under Elizabeth.

Throughout the period translation was regarded as an important labor, deserving of every encouragement. As in the sixteenth century, friends and patrons united to offer advice and aid to the author who engaged in this work. Henry Brome, dedicating a translation of Horace to Sir William Backhouse, writes of his own share of the volume, "to the translation whereof my pleasant retirement and conveniencies at your de-

---

[365]*Preface to the Reader*, in *The Natural History of C. Plinius Secundus*, London, 1601.

[366]*Dedication*, in *Ovid's Metamorphosis, Englished by G. S.*, London, 1640.

lightsome habitation have liberally contributed."[367] Doctor
Barten Holiday includes in his preface to a version of Juvenal
and Persius an interesting list of "worthy friends" who have
assisted him. "My honored friend, Mr. John Selden (of such
eminency in the studies of antiquities and languages) and Mr.
Farnaby... procured me a fair copy from the famous library of
St. James's, and a manuscript copy from our herald of learning, Mr. Camden. My dear friend, the patriarch of our poets,
Ben Jonson, sent in an ancient manuscript partly written in the
Saxon character." Then follow names of less note, Casaubon,
Anyan, Price.[368] Dryden tells the same story. He has been per-
mitted to consult the Earl of Lauderdale's manuscript translation of Virgil. "Besides this help, which was not inconsider-
able," he writes, "Mr. Congreve has done me the favor to review the *Aeneis*, and compare my version with the original."[369]
Later comes his recognition of indebtedness of a more material character. "Being invited by that worthy gentleman, Sir
William Bowyer, to Denham Court, I translated the First Geor-
gic at his house, and the greatest part of the last Aeneid. A
more friendly entertainment no man ever found... The Sev-
enth Aeneid was made English at Burleigh, the magnificent
abode of the Earl of Exeter."[370]

While private individuals thus rallied to the help of the translator, the world in general regarded his work with increasing
respect. The great Dryden thought it not unworthy of his powers to engage in putting classical verse into English garb. His
successor Pope early turned to the same pleasant and profitable task. Johnson, the literary dictator of the next age, described Rowe's version of Lucan as "one of the greatest pro-

---

[367]*Dedication*, in *The Poems of Horace rendered into Verse by Several Persons*,
London, 1666.

[368]*Juvenal and Persius*, translated by Barten Holyday, Oxford, 1673 (published
posthumously).

[369]*Dedication of the Aeneis*, in *Essays of John Dryden*, ed. W. P. Ker, v. 2, p. 235.

[370]*Postscript to the Header*, *Essays*, v. 2, p. 243.

ductions of English poetry."[371] The comprehensive editions of
the works of British poets which began to appear towards the
end of the eighteenth century regularly included English renderings, generally contemporaneous, of the great poetry of
other countries.

The growing dignity of this department of literature and the
Augustan fondness for literary criticism combined to produce
a large body of comment on methods of translation. The more
ambitious translations of the eighteenth century, for example,
were accompanied by long prefaces, containing, in addition to
the elaborate paraphernalia of contemporary scholarship, detailed discussion of the best rules for putting a foreign classic
into English. Almost every possible phase of the art had been
broached in one place and another before the century ended.
In its last decade there appeared the first attempt in English at
a complete and detailed treatment of the theory of translation
as such, Tytler's *Essay on the Principles of Translation*.

From the sixteenth-century theory of translation, so much of
which is incidental and uncertain in expression, it is a pleasure
to come to the deliberate, reasoned statements, unmistakable
in their purpose and meaning, of the earlier critics of our period, men like Denham, Cowley, and Dryden. In contrast to
the mass of unrelated individual opinions attached to the
translations of Elizabeth's time, the criticism of the seventeenth century emanates, for the most part, from a small
group of men, who supply standards for lesser commentators
and who, if they do not invariably agree with one another, are
yet thoroughly familiar with one another's views. The field of
discussion also has narrowed considerably, and theory has
gained by becoming less scattering. Translation in the seventeenth and eighteenth centuries showed certain new developments, the most marked of which was the tendency among
translators who aspired to the highest rank to confine their efforts to verse renderings of the Greek and Latin classics. A fa-

---

[371]*Rowe*, in *Lives of the Poets*, Dublin, 1804, p. 284.

vorite remark was that it is the greatest poet who suffers most in being turned from one language into another. In spite of this, or perhaps for this reason, the common ambition was to undertake Virgil, who was generally regarded as the greatest of epic poets, and attempts to translate at least a part of the *Aeneid* were astonishingly frequent. As early as 1658 the Fourth Book is described as "translated... in our day at least ten times into English."[372] Horace came next in popularity; by the beginning of the eighteenth century, according to one translator, he had been "translated, paraphrased, or criticized on by persons of all conditions and both sexes."[373] As the century progressed. Homer usurped the place formerly occupied by Virgil as the object of the most ambitious effort and the center of discussion. But there were other translations of the classics. Cooke, dedicating his translation of Hesiod to the Duke of Argyll, says to his patron: "You, my lord, know how the works of genius lift up the head of a nation above her neighbors, and give as much honor as success in arms; among these we must reckon our translations of the classics; by which when we have naturalized all Greece and Rome, we shall be so much richer than they by so many original productions as we have of our own."[374] Seemingly there was an attempt to naturalize "all Greece and Rome." Anacreon, Pindar, Apollonius Rhodius, Lucretius, Tibullus, Statius, Juvenal, Persius, Ovid, Lucan, are names taken almost at random from the list of seventeenth and eighteenth-century translations. Criticism, however, was ready to concern itself with the translation of any classic, ancient or modern. Denham's two famous pronouncements are connected, the one with his own translation of the Second Book of the *Aeneid*, the other with Sir Richard Fanshaw's rendering of *Il Pastor Fido*. In the later eighteenth

---

[372] *The Argument*, in *The Passion of Dido for Aeneas*, translated by Edmund Waller and Sidney Godolphin, London, 1668.

[373] *Dedication*, in *Translations of Horace*, John Hanway, 1730.

[374] *Dedication*, dated 1728, reprinted in *The English Poets*, London, 1810, v. 20.

century voluminous comment accompanied Hoole's *Ariosto* and Mickle's *Camoens*.

At present, however, we are concerned not with the number and variety of these translations, but with their homogeneity. As translators showed themselves less inclined to wander over the whole field of literature, the theory of translation assumed much more manageable proportions. A further limitation of the area of discussion was made by Denham, who expressly excluded from his consideration "them who deal in matters of fact or matters of faith,"[375] thus disposing of the theological treatises which had formerly divided attention with the classics.

The aims of the translator were also clarified by definition of his audience. John Vicars, publishing in 1632 *The XII. Aeneids of Virgil translated into English decasyllables,* adduces as one of his motives "the common good and public utility which I hoped might accrue to young students and grammatical tyros,"[376] but later writers seldom repeat this appeal to the learner. The next year John Brinsley issued *Virgil's Eclogues, with his book De Apibus, translated grammatically, and also according to the propriety of our English tongue so far as Grammar and the verse will permit.* A significant comment in the "Directions" runs: "As for the fear of making truants by these translations, a conceit which arose merely upon the abuse of other translations, never intended for this end, I hope that happy experience of this kind will in time drive it and all like to it utterly out of schools and out of the minds of all." Apparently the schoolmaster's ban upon the unauthorized use of translations was establishing the distinction between the English version which might claim to be ranked as literature and that which Johnson later designated as "the clandestine refuge of schoolboys."[377]

---

[375]*Preface* to *The Destruction of Troy*, in Denham, *Poems and Translations*, London, 1709.

[376]*To the courteous not curious reader.*

[377]Comment on Trapp's "blank version" of Virgil, in *Life of Dryden*.

Another limitation of the audience was, however, less admirable. For the widely democratic appeal of the Elizabethan translator was substituted an appeal to a class, distinguished, if one may believe the philosopher Hobbes, as much by social position as by intellect. In discussing the vocabulary to be employed by the translator, Hobbes professes opinions not unlike those of the sixteenth-century critics. Like Puttenham, he makes a distinction between words as suited or unsuited for the epic style. "The names of instruments and tools of artificers, and words of art," he says in the preface to his *Homer*, "though of use in the schools, are far from being fit to be spoken by a hero. He may delight in the arts themselves, and have skill in some of them, but his glory lies not in that, but in courage, nobility, and other virtues of nature, or in the command he has over other men." In Hobbes' objection to the use of unfamiliar words, also, there is nothing new; but in the standards by which he tries such terms there is something amusingly characteristic of his time. In the choice of words, "the first indiscretion is in the use of such words as to the readers of poesy (which are commonly Persons of the best Quality)"—it is only fair to reproduce Hobbes' capitalization —"are not sufficiently known. For the work of an heroic poem is to raise admiration (principally) for three virtues, valor, beauty, and love; to the reading whereof women no less than men have a just pretence though their skill in language be not so universal. And therefore foreign words, till by long use they become vulgar, are unintelligible to them." Dryden is similarly restrained by the thought of his readers. He does not try to reproduce the "Doric dialect" of Theocritus, "for Theocritus writ to Sicilians, who spoke that dialect; and I direct this part of my translations to our ladies, who neither understand, nor will take pleasure in such homely expressions."[378] In translating the *Aeneid* he follows what he conceives to have been Virgil's practice. "I will not give the reasons," he declares, "why I writ not always in the proper terms of naviga-

---

[378]Preface to *Sylvae, Essays*, v. 1, p. 266.

tion, land-service, or in the cant of any profession. I will only say that Virgil has avoided those properties, because he writ not to mariners, soldiers, astronomers, gardeners, peasants, etc., but to all in general, and in particular to men and ladies of the first quality, who have been better bred than to be too nicely knowing in such things."[379]

Another element in theory which displays the strength and weakness of the time is the treatment of the work of other countries and other periods. A changed attitude towards the achievements of foreign translators becomes evident early in the seventeenth century. In the prefaces to an edition of the works of Du Bartas in English there are signs of a growing satisfaction with the English language as a medium and an increasing conviction that England can surpass the rest of Europe in the work of translation. Thomas Hudson, in an address to James VI of Scotland, attached to his translation of *The History of Judith*, quotes an interesting conversation which he held on one occasion with that pedantic monarch. "It pleased your Highness," he recalls, "not only to esteem the peerless style of the Greek Homer and the Latin Virgil to be inimitable to us (whose tongue is barbarous and corrupted), but also to allege (partly through delight your majesty took in the haughty style of those most famous writers, and partly to sound the opinion of others) that also the lofty phrases, the grave inditement, the facund terms of the French Salust (for the like resemblance) could not be followed nor sufficiently expressed in our rough and unpolished English language."[380] It was to prove that he could reproduce the French poet "succinctly and sensibly in our vulgar speech" that Hudson undertook the *Judith*. According to the complimentary verses addressed to the famous Sylvester on his translations from the

---

[379]*Dedication of the Aeneis, Essays*, v. 2, p. 236.

[380]In *Du Bartas, His Divine Words and Works*, translated by Sylvester, London, 1641.

same author, the English tongue has responded nobly to the demands, put upon it. Sylvester has shown

> ... that French tongue's plenty to be such.
> And yet that ours can utter full as much.[381]

John Davies of Hereford, writing of another of Sylvester's translations, describes English as acquitting itself well when it competes with French, and continues

> If French to English were so strictly bound
> It would but passing lamely strive with it;
> And soon be forc'd to lose both grace and ground,
> Although they strove with equal skill and wit.[382]

An opinion characteristic of the latter part of the century is that of the Earl of Roscommon, who, after praising the work of the earlier French translators, says,

> From hence our generous emulation came,
> We undertook, and we performed the same:
> But now we show the world another way,
> And in translated verse do more than they.[383]

Dryden finds little to praise in the French and Italian renderings of Virgil. "Segrais... is wholly destitute of elevation, though his version is much better than that of the two brothers, or any of the rest who have attempted Virgil. Hannibal Caro is a great name among the Italians; yet his translation is most scandalously mean."[384] "What I have said," he declares somewhat farther on, "though it has the face of arrogance, yet is intended for the honor of my country; and therefore I will boldly own that this English translation has more of Virgil's spirit in it than either the French or Italian."[385]

---

[381]Lines by E. G., same edition.

[382]Same edition, p. 322.

[383]*An Essay on Translated Verse.*

[384]*Dedication of the Aeneis, Essays*, v. 2, p. 220.
[385]P. 222.

On translators outside their own period seventeenth-century critics bestowed even less consideration than on their French or Italian contemporaries. Earlier writers were forgotten, or remembered only to be condemned. W. L., Gent., who in 1628 published a translation of Virgil's *Eclogues*, expresses his surprise that a poet like Virgil "should yet stand still as a *noli me tangere*, whom no man either durst or would undertake; only Master Spenser long since translated the *Gnat* (a little fragment of Virgil's excellence), giving the world peradventure to conceive that he would at one time or other have gone through with the rest of this poet's work."[386] Vicars' translation of the *Aeneid* is accompanied by a letter in which the author's cousin, Thomas Vicars, congratulates him on his "great pains in transplanting this worthiest of Latin poets into a mellow and neat English soil (a thing not done before),"[387] Denham announces, "There are so few translations which deserve praise, that I scarce ever saw any which deserved pardon; those who travail in that kind being for the most part so unhappy as to rob others without enriching themselves, pulling down the fame of good authors without raising their own. Brome,[388] writing in 1666, rejoices in the good fortune of Horace's "good friend Virgil... who being plundered of all his ornaments by the old translators, was restored to others with double lustre by those standard-bearers of wit and judgment, Denham and Waller,"[389] and in proof of his statements puts side by side translations of the same passage by Phaer and Denham. Later, in 1688, an anonymous writer recalls the work of Phaer and Stanyhurst only to disparage it. Introducing his translation of Virgil, "who has so long unhappily continued a stranger to tolerable English," he says that he has "observed how *Player* and *Stainhurst* of old... had murdered the most ab-

---

[386] *To the worthy reader.*

[387] *To the courteous not curious reader*, in *The XII. Aeneids of Virgil*, 1632.

[388] Preface to *The Destruction of Troy*.

[389] Dedication of *The Poems of Horace*.

solute of poets."[390] One dissenting note is found in Robert Gould's lines prefixed to a 1687 edition of Fairfax's *Godfrey of Bulloigne*.

> See here, you dull translators, look with shame
> Upon this stately monument of fame,
> And to amaze you more, reflect how long
> It is, sines first 'twas taught the English tongue:
> In what a dark age it was brought to light;
> Dark? No, our age is dark, and that was bright.
> Of all these versions which now brightest shine,
> Most, Fairfax, are but foils to set off thine:
> Ev'n Horace can't of too much justice boast,
> His unaffected, easy style is lost:
> And Ogilby's the lumber of the stall;
> But thy translation does atone for all.[391]

Dryden, too, approves of Fairfax, considered at least as a metrist. He includes him with Spenser among the "great masters of our language," and adds, "many besides myself have heard our famous Waller own that he derived the harmony of his numbers from *Godfrey of Bulloign*, which was turned into English by Mr. Fairfax."[392] But even Dryden, who sometimes saw beyond his own period, does not share the admiration which some of his friends entertain for Chapman. "The Earl of Mulgrave and Mr. Waller," he writes in the *Examen Poeticum*, "two of the best judges of our age, have assured me that they could never read over the translation of Chapman without incredible pleasure and extreme transport. This admiration of theirs must needs proceed from the author himself, for the translator has thrown him down as far as harsh numbers, improper English, and a monstrous length of verse could carry him."[393]

---

[390] *To the Reader*, in *The First Book of Virgil's Aeneis*, London, 1688.

[391] Reprinted in *Godfrey of Bulloigne*, translated by Fairfax, New York, 1849.

[392] *Essays*, v. 2, p. 249.

[393] *Essays*, v. 2, p. 14.

In this satisfaction with their own country and their own era there lurked certain dangers for seventeenth-century writers. The quality becomes, as we shall see, more noticeable in the eighteenth century, when the shackles which English taste laid upon original poetry were imposed also upon translated verse. The theory of translation was hampered in its development by the narrow complacency of its exponents, and the record of this time is by no means one of uniform progress. The seventeenth century shows clearly marked alternations of opinion; now it sanctions extreme methods; now, by reaction, it inclines towards more moderate views. The eighteenth century, during the greater part of its course, produces little that is new in the way of theory, and adopts, without much attempt to analyze them, the formulas left by the preceding period. We may now resume the history of these developments at the point where it was dropped in Chapter III, at the end of Elizabeth's reign.

In the first part of the new century the few minor translators who described their methods held theories much like those of Chapman. W. L., Gent., in the extremely flowery and discursive preface to his version of Virgil's *Eclogues*, says, "Some readers I make no doubt they (the translations) will meet with in these dainty mouthed times, that will tax me with not coming resolved word for word and line for line with the author... I used the freedom of a translator, not tying myself to the tyranny of a grammatical construction but breaking the shell into many pieces, was only careful to preserve the kernel safe and whole from the violence of a wrong or wrested interpretation." After a long simile drawn from the hunting field he concludes, "No more do I conceive my course herein to be faulty though I do not affect to follow my author so close as to tread upon his heels." John Vicars, who professes to have robed Virgil in "a homespun English gray-coat plain," says of his manner, "I have aimed at these three things, perspicuity of the matter, fidelity to the author, and facility or smoothness to recreate thee my reader. Now if any critical or curious wit tax me with a *Frustra fit per plura &c.* and blame my not curious confinement to my author line for line, I answer (and I hope this answer will satisfy the moderate and ingenuous) that though peradventure I could (as in my Babel's Balm I have done throughout the whole translation) yet in regard of the lofty majesty of this my author's style, I would not adventure so to pinch his spirits, as to make him seem to walk like a life-less ghost. But on thinking on that of Horace, *Brevis esse laboro obscurus fio*, I presumed (yet still having an eye to the genuine sense as I was able) to expatiate with poetical liberty, where necessity of matter and phrase enforced." Vicars' warrant for his practice is the oft-quoted caution of Horace, *Nec verbum verba curabis reddere*.

But the seventeenth century was not disposed to continue un-interruptedly the tradition of previous translators. In trans-lated, as in original verse a new era was to begin, acclaimed as such in its own day, and associated like the new poetry, with the names of Denham and Cowley as both poets and critics and with that of Waller as poet. Peculiarly characteristic of the movement was its hostility towards literal translation, a hostil-ity apparent also, as we have seen, in Chapman. "I consider it a vulgar error in translating poets," writes Denham in the preface to his *Destruction of Troy*, "to affect being Fidus Inter-pres," and again in his lines to Fanshaw:

> That servile path thou nobly dost decline
> Of tracing word by word, and line by line.
> Those are the labored births of slavish brains,
> Not the effect of poetry but pains;
> Cheap, vulgar arts, whose narrowness affords
> No flight for thoughts, but poorly sticks at words.

Sprat is anxious to claim for Cowley much of the credit for in-troducing "this way of leaving verbal translations and chiefly regarding the sense and genius of the author," which "was scarce heard of in England before this present age."[394] Why

---

[394]Sprat, *Life of Cowley*, in *Prose Works of Abraham Cowley*, London, 1826.

Chapman and later translators should have fixed upon extreme literalness as the besetting fault of their predecessors and contemporaries, it is hard to see. It is true that the recognition of the desirability of faithfulness to the original was the most distinctive contribution that sixteenth-century critics made to the theory of translation, but this principle was largely associated with prose renderings of a different type from that now under discussion. If, like Denham, one excludes "matters of fact and matters of faith," the body of translation which remains is scarcely distinguished by slavish adherence to the letter. As a matter of fact, however, sixteenth-century translation was obviously an unfamiliar field to most seventeenth-century commentators, and although their generalizations include all who have gone before them, their illustrations are usually drawn from the early part of their own century. Ben Jonson, whose translation of Horace's *Art of Poetry* is cited by Dry den as an example of "metaphrase, or turning an author word by word and line by line from one language to another,"[395] is perhaps largely responsible for the mistaken impression regarding the earlier translators. Thomas May and George Sandys are often included in the same category. Sandys' translation of Ovid is regarded by Dryden as typical of its time. Its literalism, its resulting lack of poetry, "proceeded from the wrong judgment of the age in which he lived. They neither knew good verse nor loved it; they were scholars, 'tis true, but they were pedants; and for all their pedantic pains, all their translations want to be translated into English."[396]

---

[395]*Preface to the Translation of Ovid's Epistles, Essays*, v. 1, p. 237.

[396]*Dedication of Examen Poeticum, Essays*, v. 2, p. 10. Johnson, writing of the latter part of the seventeenth century, says, "The authority of Jonson, Sandys, and Holiday had fixed the judgment of the nation" {*The Idler*, 69), and Tytler, in his *Essay on the Principles of Translation*, 1791, says, "In poetical translation the English writers of the sixteenth, and the greatest part of the seventeenth century, seem to have had no other care than (in Denham's phrase) to translate language into language, and to have placed their whole merit in presenting a literal and servile transcript of their original."

But neither Jonson, Sandys, nor May has much to say with regard to the proper methods of translation. The most definite utterance of the group is found in the lines which Jonson addressed to May on his translation of Lucan:

> But who hath them interpreted, and brought
> Lucan's whole frame unto us, and so wrought
> As not the smallest joint or gentlest word
> In the great mass or machine there is stirr'd?
> The self same genius I so the world will say
> The sun translated, or the son of May.[397]

May's own preface says nothing of his theories. Sandys says of his Ovid, "To the translation I have given what perfection my pen could bestow, by polishing, altering, or restoring the harsh, improper, or mistaken with a nicer exactness than perhaps is required in so long a labor,"[398] a comment open to various interpretations. His metrical version of the Psalms is described as "paraphrastically translated," and it is worthy of note that Cowley, in his attack on the practice of too literal translation, should have chosen this part of Sandys' work as illustrative of the methods which he condemns. For the translators of the new school, though professedly the foes of the word for word method, carried their hostility to existing theories of translation much farther. Cowley begins, reasonably enough, by pointing out the absurdity of translating a poet literally. "If a man should undertake to translate Pindar word for word, it would be thought that one madman had translated another; as may appear when a person who understands not the original reads the verbal traduction of him into Latin prose, than which nothing seems more raving… And I would gladly know what applause our best pieces of English poesy could expect from a Frenchman or Italian, if converted faithfully and word for word into French or Italian prose."[399] But,

---

[397] In Lucan's *Pharsalia*, translated May, 1659.

[398] *To the Reader*, in *Ovid's Metamorphosis*, translated Sandys, London, 1640.
[399] *Preface to Pindaric Odes*, reprinted in *Essays and other Prose Writings*, Oxford, 1915.

ignoring the possibility of a reasonable regard for both the
original and the English, such as had been advocated by
Chapman or by minor translators like W. L. and Vicars, Cowley suggests a more radical method. Since of necessity much
of the beauty of a poem is lost in translation, the translator
must supply new beauties. "For men resolving in no case to
shoot beyond the mark," he says, "it is a thousand to one if
they shoot not short of it." "We must needs confess that after
all these losses sustained by Pindar, all we can add to him by
our wit or invention (not deserting still his subject) is not
likely to make him a richer man than he was in his own country." Finally comes a definite statement of Cowley's method:
"Upon this ground I have in these two Odes of Pindar taken,
left out and added what I please; nor make it so much my aim
to let the reader know precisely what he spoke as what was
his way and manner of speaking, which has not been yet (that
I know of) introduced into English, though it be the noblest
and highest kind of writing in verse." Denham, in his lines on
Fanshaw's translation of Guarini, had already approved of a
similar method:

> A new and nobler way thou dost pursue
> To make translations and translators too.
> They but preserve the ashes, thou the flame,
> True to his sense, but truer to his fame.
> Feeding his current, where thou find'st it low
> Let'st in thine own to make it rise and flow;
> Wisely restoring whatsoever grace
> Is lost by change of times, or tongues, or place.

Denham, however, justifies the procedure for reasons which
must have had their appeal for the translator who was conscious of real creative power. "Poesy," he says in the preface
to his translation from the *Aeneid*, "is of so subtle a spirit that
in the pouring out of one language into another it will all
evaporate; and if a new spirit be not added m transfusion,
there will remain nothing but a *caput mortuum*." The new

method, which Cowley is willing to designate as *imitation* if the critics refuse to it the name of translation, is described by Dryden with his usual clearness. "I take imitation of an author in their sense," he says, "to be an endeavor of a later poet to write like one who has written before him, on the same subject; that is, not to translate his words, or be confined to his sense, but only to set him as a pattern, and to write as he supposes that author would have done, had he lived in our age, and in our country."[400]

Yet, after all, the new fashion was far from revolutionizing either the theory or the practice of translation. Dryden says of Denham that "he advised more liberty than he took himself," and of both Denham and Cowley, "I dare not say that either of them have carried this libertine way of rendering authors (as Mr Cowley calls it) so far as my definition reaches; for in the *Pindaric Odes* the customs and ceremonies of ancient Greece are still observed."[401] In the theory of the less distinguished translators of the second and third quarters of the century, the influence of Denham and Cowley shows itself, if at all, in the claim to have translated paraphrastically and the complacency with which translators describe their practice as "new," a condition of things which might have prevailed without the intervention of the method of imitation. About the year 1680 there comes a definite reaction against too great liberty in the treatment of foreign authors. Thomas Creech, defining what may justly be expected of the translator of Horace, says, "If the sense of the author is delivered, the variety of expression kept (which I must despair of after Quintillian hath assured us that he is most happily bold in his words) and his fancy not debauched (for I cannot think myself able to improve Horace) 'tis all that can be expected from a version."[402] After quoting with approval what Cowley has said of the inadequacy of any

---

[400] *Preface to Ovid's Epistles, Essays*, v. 1, p. 239.

[401] Pp. 239-40.
[402] *Dedication to Dryden*, 1684, in *The Odes, Satires, and Epistles of Horace done into English*, London, 1688.

translation, he continues: "'Tis true he (Cowley) improves this consideration, and urges it as concluding against all strict and faithful versions, in which I must beg leave to dissent, thinking it better to convey down the learning of the ancients than their empty sound suited to the present times, and show the age their whole substance, rather than their ghost embodied in some light air of my own." An anonymous writer presents a group of critics who are disgusted with contemporary fashions in translation and wish to go back to those which prevailed in the early part of the century.[403]

> Acer, incensed, exclaimed against the age,
> Said some of our new poets had of late
> Set up a lazy fashion to translate,
> Speak authors how they please, and if they call
> Stuff they make paraphrase, that answers all.
> Pedantic verse, effeminately smooth,
> Racked through all little rules of art to soothe,
> The soft'ned age industriously compile,
> Main wit and cripple fancy all the while.
> A license far beyond poetic use
> Not to translate old authors but abuse
> The wit of Romans; and their lofty sense
> Degrade into new poems made from thence,
> Disguise old Rome in our new eloquence.

Aesculape shares the opinion of Acer.

> And thought it fit wits should be more confined
> To author's sense, and to their periods too,
> Must leave out nothing, every sense must do,
> And though they cannot render verse for verse,
> Yet every period's sense they must rehearse.

---

[403]*Metellus his Dialogues, Relation of a Journey to Tunbridge Wells, with the Fourth Book of Virgil's Aeneid in English*, London, 1693.

Finally Metellus, speaking for the group, orders Laelius, one of their number, to translate the Fourth Book of the *Aeneid*, keeping himself in due subordination to Virgil.

> We all bid then translate it the old way
> Not a-la-mode, but like George Sandys or May;
> Show Virgil's every period, not steal sense
> To make up a new-fashioned poem thence.

Other translators, though not defending the literal method, do not advocate imitation. Roscommon, in the *Essay on Translated Verse*, demands fidelity to the substance of the original when he says,

> The genuine sense, intelligibly told,
> Shows a translator both discreet and bold.
> Excursions are inexpiably bad,
> And 'tis much safer to leave out than add,

but, unlike Phaer, he forbids the omission of difficult passages:

> Abstruse and mystic thoughts you must express,
> With painful care and seeming easiness.

Dryden considers the whole situation in detail.[404] He admires Cowley's *Pindaric Odes* and admits that both Pindar and his translator do not come under ordinary rules, but he fears the effect of Cowley's example "when writers of unequal parts to him shall imitate so bold an undertaking," and believes that only a poet so "wild and ungovernable" as Pindar justifies the method of Cowley. "If Virgil, or Ovid, or any regular intelligible authors be thus used, 'tis no longer to be called their work, when neither the thoughts nor words are drawn from the original; but instead of them there is something new produced, which is almost the creation of another hand... He who is inquisitive to know an author's thoughts will be disappointed in his expectation; and 'tis not always that a man will be contented to have a present made him, when he expects the payment of a debt. To state it fairly; imitation is the most ad-

---

[404] *Preface to the Translation of Ovid's Epistles, Essays*, vol. 1, p. 240.

vantageous way for a translator to show himself, but the greatest wrong which can be done to the memory and reputation of the dead."

Though imitation was not generally accepted as a standard method of translation, certain elements in the theory of Denham and Cowley remained popular throughout the seventeenth and even the eighteenth century. A favorite comment in the complimentary verses attached to translations is the assertion that the translator has not only equaled but surpassed his original. An extreme example of this is Dryden's fatuous reference to the Earl of Mulgrave's translation of Ovid:

> How will sweet Ovid's ghost be pleased to hear
> His fame augmented by an English peer,
> How he embellishes his Helen's loves,
> Outdoes his softness, and his sense improves.[405]

His earlier lines to Sir Robert Howard on the latter's translation of the *Achilleis* of Statius are somewhat less bald:

> To understand how much we owe to you,
> We must your numbers with your author's view;
> Then shall we see his work was lamely rough,
> Each figure stiff as if designed in buff;
> His colours laid so thick on every place,
> As only showed the paint, but hid the face;
> But as in perspective we beauties see
> Which in the glass, not in the picture be,
> So here our sight obligingly mistakes
> That wealth which his your bounty only makes.
> Thus vulgar dishes are by cooks disguised,
> More for their dressing than their substance prized.[406]

It was especially in cases where the original lacked smoothness and perspicuity, the qualities which appealed most strongly to the century, that the claim to improvement was

---

[405] *To the Earl of Roscommon on his excellent Essay on Translated Verse.*
[406] In Sir Robert Howard's *Poems*, London, 1660.

made. Often, however, it was associated with notably accurate versions. Cartwright calls upon the readers of Holiday's *Persius*,

> who when they shall view
> How truly with thine author thou dost pace,
> How hand in hand ye go, what equal grace
> Thou dost observe with him in every term,
> They cannot but, if just, justly affirm
> That did your times as do your lines agree,
> He might be thought to have translated thee,
> But that he's darker, not so strong; wherein
> Thy greater art more clearly may be seen,
> Which does thy Persius' cloudy storms display
> With lightning and with thunder; both which lay
> Couched perchance in him, but wanted force
> To break, or light from darkness to divorce,
> Till thine exhaled skill compressed it so,
> That forced the clouds to break, the light to show,
> The thunder to be heard. That now each child
> Can prattle what was meant; whilst thou art styled
> Of all, with titles of true dignity
> For lofty phrase and perspicuity.[407]

J. A. addresses Lucretius in lines prefixed to Creech's translation,

> But Lord, how much you're changed, how much improv'd!
> Your native roughness all is left behind,
> But still the same good man tho' more refin'd,[408]

and Otway says to the translator:

> For when the rich original we peruse,
> And by it try the metal you produce,
> Though there indeed the purest ore we find,

---

[407] In Holiday's *Persius*, Fifth Edition, 1650.
[408] In Creech's *Lucretius*, Third Edition, Oxford, 1683.

> Yet still by you it something is refined;
> Thus when the great Lucretius gives a loose
> And lashes to her speed his fiery Muse,
> Still with him you maintain an equal pace,
> And bear full stretch upon him all the race;
> But when in rugged way we find him rein
> His verse, and not so smooth a stroke maintain,
> There the advantage he receives is found,
> By you taught temper, and to choose his ground.[409]

So authoritative a critic as Roscommon, however, seems to oppose attempts at improvement when he writes,

> Your author always will the best advise,
> Fall when he falls, and when he rises, rise,

a precept which Tytler, writing at the end of the next century, considers the one doubtful rule in *The Essay on Translated Verse*. "Far from adopting the former part of this maxim," he declares, "I consider it to be the duty of a poetical translator, never to suffer his original to fall. He must maintain with him a perpetual contest of genius; he must attend him in his highest flights, and soar, if he can, beyond him: and when he perceives, at any time a diminution of his powers, when he sees a drooping wing, he must raise him on his own pinions."[410]

The influence of Denham and Cowley is also seen in what is perhaps the most significant element in the seventeenth-century theory of translation. These men advocated freedom in translation, not because such freedom would give the translator a greater opportunity to display his own powers, but because it would enable him to reproduce more truly the spirit of the original. A good translator must, first of all, know his author intimately. Where Denham's expressions are fuller than Virgil's, they are, he says, "but the impressions which the often reading of him hath left upon my thoughts." Possessing

---

[409]In Creech's Lucretius, Third Edition, Oxford, 1683.

[410]*Essay on the Principles of Translation*, Everyman's Library, pp. 46-6.

this intimate acquaintance, the English writer must try to think and write as if he were identified with his author. Dryden, who, in spite of his general principles, sometimes practised something uncommonly like imitation, says in the preface to *Sylvae*: "I must acknowledge that I have many times exceeded my commission; for I have both added and omitted, and even sometimes very boldly made such expositions of my authors as no Dutch commentator will forgive me... Where I have enlarged them, I desire the false critics would not always think that those thoughts are wholly mine, but either that they are secretly in the poet, or may be fairly deduced from him; or at least, if both these considerations should fail, that my own is of a piece with his, and that if he were living, and an Englishman, they are such as he would probably have written."[411]

By a sort of irony the more faithful translator came in time to recognize this as one of the precepts of his art, and sometimes to use it as an argument against too much liberty. The Earl of Roscommon says in the preface to his translation of Horace's *Art of Poetry*, "I have kept as close as I could both to the meaning and the words of the author, and done nothing but what I believe he would forgive if he were alive; and I have often asked myself this question." Dryden follows his protest against imitation by saying: "Nor must we understand the language only of the poet, but his particular turn of thoughts and expression, which are the characters that distinguish, and, as it were, individuate him from all other writers. When we come thus far, 'tis time to look into ourselves, to conform our genius to his, to give his thought either the same turn, if our tongue will bear it, or if not, to vary but the dress, not to alter or destroy the substance."[412] Such faithfulness, according to Dryden, involves the appreciation and the reproduction of the qualities in an author which distinguish him from others, or, to use his own words, "the maintaining the character of an au-

---

[411]*Essays*, v. 1, p. 252.
[412]*Preface to the Translation of Ovid's Epistles, Essays*, v. 1, p. 241.

thor which distinguishes him from all others, and makes him appear that individual poet whom you would interpret."[413] Dryden thinks that English translators have not sufficiently recognized the necessity for this. "For example, not only the thoughts, but the style and versification of Virgil and Ovid are very different: yet I see, even in our best poets who have translated some parts of them, that they have confounded their several talents, and, by endeavoring only at the sweetness and harmony of numbers, have made them so much alike that, if I did not know the originals, I should never be able to judge by the copies which was Virgil and which was Ovid. It was objected against a late noble painter that he drew many graceful pictures, but few of them were like. And this happened because he always studied himself more than those who sat to him. In such translators I can easily distinguish the hand which performed the work, but I cannot distinguish their poet from another."

But critics recognized that study and pains alone could not furnish the translator for his work. "To be a thorough translator," says Dryden, "he must be a thorough poet,"[414] or to put it, as does Roscommon, somewhat more mildly, he must by nature possess the more essential characteristics of his author. Admitting this, Creech writes with a slight air of apology, "I cannot choose but smile to think that I, who have… too little ill nature (for that is commonly thought a necessary ingredient) to be a satirist, should venture upon Horace."[415] Dryden finds by experience that he can more easily translate a poet akin to himself. His translations of Ovid please him. "Whether it be the partiality of an old man to his youngest child I know not; but they appear to me the best of all my endeavors in this kind. Perhaps this poet is more easy to be translated than some others whom I have lately attempted; perhaps, too, he

---

[413]*Preface to Sylvae, Essays*, v. 1, p. 254.

[414]*Ibid.*, p. 264.

[415]*Preface*, in Second Edition of *Odes of Horace*, London, 1688.

was more according to my genius."[416] He looks forward with pleasure to putting the whole of the *Iliad* into English. "And this I dare assure the world beforehand, that I have found, by trial, Homer a more pleasing task than Virgil, though I say not the translation will be less laborious; for the Grecian is more according to my genius than the Latin poet."[417] The insistence on the necessity for kinship between the author and the translator is the principal idea in Roscommon's *Essay on Translated Verse*. According to Roscommon,

> Each poet with a different talent writes,
> One praises, one instructs, another bites.
> Horace could ne'er aspire to epic bays,
> Nor lofty Maro stoop to lyric lays.

This, then, is his advice to the would-be translator:

> Examine how your humour is inclined,
> And which the ruling passion of your mind;
> Then, seek a poet who your way does bend,
> And choose an author as you choose a friend.
> United by this sympathetic bond,
> You grow familiar, intimate, and fond;
> Your thoughts, your words, your styles, your souls agree,
> No longer his interpreter but he.

Though the plea of reproducing the spirit of the original was sometimes made a pretext for undue latitude, it is evident that there was here an important contribution to the theory of translation. In another respect, also, the consideration of metrical effects, the seventeenth century shows some advance, — an advance, however, which must be laid chiefly to the credit of Dryden. Apparently there was no tendency towards innovation and experiment in the matter of verse forms. Seventeenth-century translators, satisfied with the couplet and kin-

---

[416]*Examen Poeticum, Essays*, v. 2, p. 9.

[417]*Preface to the Fables, Essays*, v, 2, p. 251.

dred measures, did not consider, as the Elizabethans had done, the possibility of introducing classical metres. Creech says of Horace, "'Tis certain our language is not capable of the numbers of the poet,"[418] and leaves the matter there. Holiday says of his translation of the same poet: "But many, no doubt, will say Horace is by me forsaken, his lyric softness and emphatical Muse maimed; that there is a general defection from his genuine harmony. Those I must tell, I have in this translation rather sought his spirit than numbers; yet the music of verse not neglected neither, since the English ear better heareth the distich, and findeth that sweetness and air which the Latin affecteth and (questionless) attaineth in sapphics or iambic measures."[419] Dryden frequently complains of the difficulty of translation into English metre, especially when the poet to be translated is Virgil. The use of rhyme causes trouble. It "is certainly a constraint even to the best poets, and those who make it with most ease… What it adds to sweetness, it takes away from sense; and he who loses the least by it may be called a gainer. It often makes us swerve from an author's meaning; as, if a mark be set up for an archer at a great distance, let him aim as exactly as he can, the least wind will take his arrow, and divert it from the white."[420] The line of the heroic couplet is not long enough to reproduce the hexameter, and Virgil is especially succinct. "To make him copious is to alter his character; and to translate him line for line is impossible, because the Latin is naturally a more succinct language than either the Italian, Spanish, French, or even than the English, which, by reason of its monosyllables, is far the most compendious of them. Virgil is much the closest of any Roman poet, and the Latin hexameter has more feet than the English heroic."[421] Yet though Dryden admits that Caro, the Italian translator, who used blank verse, made his task easier thereby,

---

[418]*To the Reader*, in *The Odes, Satires, and Epistles of Horace*, London, 1688.

[419]*Preface* to translation of Horace, 1652.

[420]*Dedication of the Eneis*, *Essays*, v. 2, pp. 220-1.

[421]*Preface to Sylvae*, *Essays*, v. 1, pp. 256-7.

he does not think of abandoning the couplet for any of the verse forms which earlier translators had tried. He finds Chapman's *Homer* characterized by "harsh numbers… and a monstrous length of verse," and thinks his own period "a much better age than was the last… for versification and the art of numbers."[422] Roscommon, whose version of Horace's *Art of Poetry* is in blank verse, says that Jonson's translation lacks clearness as a result not only of his literalness but of "the constraint of rhyme,"[423] but makes no further attack on the couplet as the regular vehicle for translation.

Dryden, however, is peculiarly interested in the general effect of his verse as compared with that of his originals. "I have attempted," he says in the *Examen Poeticum*, "to restore Ovid to his native sweetness, easiness, and smoothness, and to give my poetry a kind of cadence and, as we call it, a run of verse, as like the original as the English can come to the Latin."[424] In his study of Virgil previous to translating the *Aeneid* he observed "above all, the elegance of his expressions and the harmony of his numbers."[425] Elsewhere he says of his author, "His verse is everywhere sounding the very thing in your ears whose sense it bears, yet the numbers are perpetually varied to increase the delight of the reader; so that the same sounds are never repeated twice together."[426] These metrical effects he has tried to reproduce in English. "The turns of his verse, his breakings, his numbers, and his gravity, I have as far imitated as the poverty of our language and the hastiness of my performance would allow," he says in the preface to *Sylvae*.[427] In his translation of the whole *Aeneid* he was guided by the same considerations. "Virgil… is everywhere elegant, sweet, and

---

[422] *Examen Poeticum, Essays*, v. 2, p. 14.

[423] *Preface.*

[424] *Essays*, v. 2, p. 10.

[425] *Dedication of the Eneis, Essays*, v. 2, p. 223.

[426] *Preface to Sylvae, Essays*, v. 1, p. 255.

[427] *Essays*, v. 1, p. 258.

flowing in his hexameters. His words are not only chosen, but the places in which he ranks them for the sound. He who removes them from the station wherein their master set them spoils the harmony. What he says of the Sibyl's prophecies may be as properly applied to every word of his: they must be read in order as they he; the least breath discomposes them and somewhat of their divinity is lost. I cannot boast that I have been thus exact in my verses; but I have endeavored to follow the example of my master, and am the first Englishman, perhaps, who made it his design to copy him in his numbers, his choice of words, and his placing them for the sweetness of the sound. On this last consideration I have shunned the caesura as much as possibly I could: for, wherever that is used, it gives a roughness to the verse; of which we have little need in a language which is overstocked with consonants."[428] Views like these contribute much to an adequate conception of what faithfulness in translation demands.

From the lucid, intelligent comment of Dryden it is disappointing to turn to the body of doctrine produced by his successors. In spite of the widespread interest in translation during the eighteenth century, little progress was made in formulating the theory of the art, and many of the voluminous prefaces of translators deserve the criticism which Johnson applied to Garth, "his notions are half-formed." So far as concerns the general method of translation, the principles laid down by critics are often mere repetitions of the conclusions already reached in the preceding century. Most theorists were ready to adopt Dryden's view that the translator should strike a middle course between the very free and the very close method. Put into words by a recognized authority, so reasonable an opinion could hardly fail of acceptance. It appealed to the eighteenth-century mind as adequate, and more than one translator, professing to give rules for translation, merely repeated in his own words what Dryden had already said. Garth declares in the preface condemned by Johnson: "Trans-

---

[428] *Dedication of the Eneis, Essays*, v. 2, p. 215.

lation is commonly either verbal, a paraphrase, or an imitation… The manner that seems most suitable for this present undertaking is neither to follow the author too close out of a critical timorousness, nor abandon him too wantonly through a poetic boldness. The original should always be kept in mind, without too apparent a deviation from the sense. Where it is otherwise, it is not a version but an imitation."[429] Grainger says in the introduction to his *Tibullus*: "Verbal translations are always inelegant, because always destitute of beauty of idiom and language; for by their fidelity to an author's words, they become treacherous to his reputation; on the other hand, a too wanton departure from the letter often varies the sense and alters the manner. The translator chose the middle way, and meant neither to tread on the heels of Tibullus nor yet to lose sight of him."[430] The preface to Fawkes' *Theocritus* harks back to Dryden: "A too faithful translation, Mr. Dryden says, must be a pedantic one… And as I have not endeavored to give a verbal translation, so neither have I indulged myself in a rash paraphrase, which always loses the spirit of an ancient by degenerating into the modern manners of expression."[431]

Yet behind these well-sounding phrases there lay, one suspects, little vigorous thought. Both the clarity and the honesty which belong to Dryden's utterances are absent from much of the comment of the eighteenth century. The apparent judicial impartiality of Garth, Fawkes, Grainger, and their contemporaries disappears on closer examination. In reality the balance of opinion in the time of Pope and Johnson inclines very perceptibly in favor of freedom. Imitation, it is true, soon ceases to enter into the discussion of translation proper, but literalism is attacked again and again, till one is ready to ask, with Dryden, "Who defends it?" Mickle's preface to *The Lusiad* states with unusual frankness what was probably the underlying

---

[429]In *Ovid's Metamorphoses translated by Dryden, Addison, Garth, etc.*, reprinted in *The English Poets*, v. 20.

[430]*Advertisement* to *Elegies of Tibullus*, reprinted in same volume.

[431]*Preface* to *Idylliums of Theocritus*, reprinted in same volume.

idea in most of the theory of the time. Writing "not to gratify the dull few, whose greatest pleasure is to see what the author exactly says," but "to give a poem that might live in the English language," Mickle puts up a vigorous defense of his methods. "Literal translation of poetry," he insists, "is a solecism. You may construe your author, indeed, but if with some translators you boast that you have left your author to speak for himself, that you have neither added nor diminished, you have in reality grossly abused him, and deceived yourself. Your literal translations can have no claim to the original felicities of expression, the energy, elegance, and fire of the original poetry. It may bear, indeed, a resemblance, but such an one as a corpse in the sepulchre bears to the former man, when he moved in the bloom and vigor of life.

> Nec verbum verbo curabis reddere, fidus
> Interpres—

was the taste of the Augustan age. None but a poet can translate a poet. The freedom which this precept gives will, therefore, in a poet's hands, not only infuse the energy, elegance, and fire of the author's poetry into his own version, but will give it also the spirit of an original."[432] A similarly clear statement of the real facts of the situation appears in Johnson's remarks on translators. His test for a translation is its readability, and to attain this quality he thinks it permissible for the translator to improve on his author. "To a thousand cavils," he writes in the course of his comments on Pope's *Homer*, "one answer is necessary; the purpose of a writer is to be read, and the criticism which would destroy the power of pleasing must be blown aside."[433] The same view comes forward in his estimate of Cowley's work. "The Anacreon of Cowley, like the Homer of Pope, has admitted the decoration of some modern graces, by which he is undoubtedly more amiable to common readers, and perhaps, if they would honestly declare their

---

[432]*Dissertation on The Lusiad*, reprinted in *The English Poets*, v. 21.

[433]*Pope*, in *Lives of the Poets*, p. 568.

own perceptions, to far the greater part of those whom courtesy and ignorance are content to style the learned."[434]

In certain matters, however, the translator claimed especial freedom. "A work of this nature," says Trapp of his translation of the *Aeneid*, "is to be regarded in two different views, both as a poem and as a translated poem." This gives the translator some latitude. "The thought and contrivance are his author's, but his language and the turn of his versification are his own."[435] Pope holds the same opinion. A translator must "give his author entire and unmaimed" but for the rest the diction and versification are his own province.[436] Such a dictum was sure to meet with approval, for dignity of language and smoothness of verse were the very qualities on which the period prided itself. It was in these respects that translators hoped to improve on the work of the preceding age. Fawkes, the translator of Theocritus, believes that many lines in Dryden's *Miscellany* "will sound very harshly in the polished ears of the present age," and that Creech's translation of his author can be popular only with those who "having no ear for poetical numbers, are better pleased with the rough music of the last age than the refined harmony of this." Johnson, who strongly approved of Dryden's performance, accepts it as natural that there should be other attempts at the translation of Virgil, "since the English ear has been accustomed to the mellifluence of Pope's numbers, and the diction of poetry has become more splendid."[437] There was something of poetic justice in this attitude towards the seventeenth century, itself so unappreciative of the achievements of earlier translators, but exemplified in practice, it showed the peculiar limitations of the age of Pope.

---

[434] *Cowley*, in *Lives*, p. 25.

[435] Preface of 1718, reprinted in *The Works of Virgil translated into English blank verse by Joseph Trapp*, London, 1735.

[436] *Preface to Homer's Iliad.*

[437] *Dryden* in *Lives of the Poets*, p. 226.

As in the seventeenth century, the heroic couplet was the pre-
dominant form in translations. Blank verse, when employed,
was generally associated with a protest against the prevailing
methods of translators. Trapp and Brady, both of whom early
in the century attempted blank verse renderings of the *Aeneid*,
justify their use of this form on the ground that it permits
greater faithfulness to the original. Brady intends to avoid the
rock upon which other translators have split, "and that seems
to me to be their translating this noble and elegant poet into
rhyme; by which they were sometimes forced to abandon the
sense, and at other times to cramp it very much, which inconveniences may probably be avoided in blank verse."[438] Trapp
makes a more violent onslaught upon earlier translations,
which he finds "commonly so very licentious that they can
scarce be called so much as paraphrases," and presents the
employment of blank verse as in some degree a remedy for
this. "The fetters of rhyme often cramp the expression and
spoil the verse, and so you can both translate more closely and
also more fully express the spirit of your author without it
than with it."[439] Neither version however was kindly received,
and though there continued to be occasional efforts to break
away from what Warton calls "the Gothic shackles of
rhyme"[440] or from the oversmoothness of Augustan verse, the
more popular translators set the stamp of their approval on
the couplet in its classical perfection. Grainger, who translated
Tibullus, discusses the possibility of using the "alternate"
stanza, but ends by saying that he has generally "preferred the
heroic measure, which is not better suited to the lofty sound of
the epic muse than to the complaining tone of the elegy."[441]
Hoole chooses the couplet for his version of Ariosto, because it
occupies the same place in English that the octave stanza occupies in Italian, and because it is capable of great variety. "Of

---

[438] *Proposals for a translation of Virgil's Aeneis in Blank Verse*, London, 1713.

[439] *Preface, op. cit.*

[440] *Prefatory Dedication*, in *The Works of Virgil in English Verse*, London, 1763.

[441] *Advertisement, op. cit.*

all the various styles used by the best poets," he says, "none seems so well adapted to the mixed and familiar narrative as that of Dryden in his last production, known by the name of his *Fables*, which by their harmony, spirit, ease, and variety of versification, exhibit an admirable model for a translation of Ariosto."[442] It was, however, to the regularity of Pope's couplet that most translators aspired. Francis, the translator of Horace, who succeeded in pleasing his readers in spite of his failure to conform with popular standards, puts the situation well in a comment which recalls a similar utterance of Dryden. "The misfortune of our translators," he says, "is that they have only one style; and consequently all their authors, Homer, Virgil, Horace, and Ovid, are compelled to speak in the same numbers, and the same unvaried expression. The free-born spirit of poetry is confined in twenty constant syllables, and the sense regularly ends with every second line, as if the writer had not strength enough to support himself or courage enough to venture into a third."[443]

Revolts against the couplet, then, were few and generally unsuccessful. Prose translations of the epic, such as have in our own day attained some popularity, were in the eighteenth century regarded with especial disfavor. It was known that they had some vogue in France, but that was not considered a recommendation. The English translation of Madame Dacier's prose Homer, issued by Ozell, Oldisworth, and Broome, was greeted with scorn. Trapp, in the preface to his Virgil, refers to the new French fashion with true insular contempt. Segrais' translation is "almost as good as the French language will allow, which is just as fit for an epic poem as an ambling nag is for a war horse... Their language is excellent for prose, but quite otherwise for verse, especially heroic. And therefore tho' the translating of poems into prose is a strange modern invention, yet the French transprosers are so far in the right because

---

[442]*Preface* to *Ariosto*, reprinted in *The English Poets*, v. 21.

[443]*Preface*, reprinted in *The English Poets*, v. 19.

their language will not bear verse." Mickle, mentioning in his *Dissertation on the Lusiad* that "M. Duperron de Castera, in 1735, gave in French prose a loose unpoetical paraphrase of the Lusiad," feels it necessary to append in a note his opinion that "a literal prose translation of poetry is an attempt as absurd as to translate fire into water."

If there was little encouragement for the translator to experiment with new solutions of the problems of versification, there was equally little latitude allowed him in the other division of his peculiar province, diction. In accordance with existing standards, critics doubled their insistence on Decorum, a quality in which they found the productions of former times lacking. Johnson criticizes Dryden's *Juvenal* on the ground that it wants the dignity of its original.[444] Fawkes finds Creech "more rustic than any of the rustics in the Sicilian bard," and adduces in proof many illustrations, from his calling a "noble pastoral cup a fine two-handled pot" to his dubbing his characters "Tawney Bess, Tom, Will, Dick" in vulgar English style.[445] Fanshaw, says Mickle in the preface to his translation of Camoens, had not "the least idea of the dignity of the epic style." The originals themselves, however, presented obstacles to suitable rendering. Preston finds this so in the case of Apollonius Rhodius, and offers this, explanation of the matter: "Ancient terms of art, even if they can be made intelligible, cannot be rendered, with any degree of grace, into a modern language, where the corresponding terms are debased into vulgarity by low and familiar use. Many passages of this kind are to be found in Homer. They are frequent also in Apollonius Rhodius; particularly so, from the exactness which he affects in describing everything."[446] Warton, unusually tolerant of Augustan taste in this respect, finds the same difficulty in the *Eclogues* and *Georgics* of Virgil. "A poem whose excellence peculiarly consists in the graces of diction," his preface runs,

---

[444]*Dryden*, in *Lives*, p. 226.

[445]*Op. cit.*

[446]*Preface*, reprinted in *The British Poets*, Chiswick, 1822, v. 90.

"is far more difficult to be translated, than a work where senti-
ment, or passion, or imagination is chiefly displayed... Besides, the meanness of the terms of husbandry is concealed
and lost in a dead language, and they convey no low and despicable image to the mind; but the coarse and common words
I was necessitated to use in the following translation, viz.
plough and sow, wheat, dung, ashes, horse and cow, etc., will, I
fear, unconquerably disgust many a delicate reader, if he doth
not make proper allowance for a modern compared with an
ancient language."[447] According to Hoole, the English language confines the translator within narrow limits. A translation of Berni's *Orlando Innamorato* into English verse would be
almost impossible, "the narrative descending to such familiar
images and expressions as would by no means suit the genius
of our language and poetry."[448] The task of translating Ariosto,
though not so hopeless, is still arduous on this account. "There
is a certain easy negligence in his muse that often assumes a
playful mode of expression incompatible with the nature of
our present poetry... An English translator will have frequent
reason to regret the more rigid genius of the language, that
rarely permits him in this respect, to attempt even an imitation
of his author."

The comments quoted in the preceding pages make one realize that, while the translator was left astonishingly free as regarded his treatment of the original, it was at his peril that he
ran counter to contemporary literary standards. The discussion centering around Pope's *Homer*, at once the most popular
and the most typical translation of the period, may be taken as
presenting the situation in epitome. Like other prefaces of the
time, Pope's introductory remarks are, whether intentionally
or unintentionally, misleading. He begins, in orthodox fashion, by advocating the middle course approved by Dryden. "It
is certain," he writes, "no literal translation can be just to an

---

[447]*Prefatory Dedication*, in *The Works of Virgil in English Verse*, London, 1763.

[448]*Preface to Ariosto*, reprinted in *The English Poets*, v. 21.

excellent original in a superior language: but it is a great mistake to imagine (as many have done) that a rash paraphrase can make amends for this general defect; which is no less in danger to lose the spirit of an ancient, by deviating into the modern manners of expression." Continuing, however, he urges an unusual degree of faithfulness. The translator must not think of improving upon his author. "I will venture to say," he declares, "there have not been more men misled in former times by a servile, dull adherence to the letter, than have been deluded in ours by a chimerical insolent hope of raising and improving their author... 'Tis a great secret in writing to know when to be plain, and when poetical and figurative; and it is what Homer will teach us, if we will but follow modestly in his footsteps. Where his diction is bold and lofty, let us raise ours as high as we can; but where his is plain and humble, we ought not to be deterred from imitating him by the fear of incurring the censure of a mere English critic." The translator ought to endeavor to "copy him in all the variations of his style, and the different modulations of his numbers; to preserve, in the more active or descriptive parts, a warmth and elevation; in the more sedate or narrative, a plainness and solemnity; in the speeches a fullness and perspicuity; in the sentences a shortness and gravity: not to neglect even the little figures and turns on the words, nor sometimes the very cast of the periods; neither to omit nor confound any rites and customs of antiquity."

Declarations like this would, if taken alone, make one rate Pope as a pioneer in the art of translation. Unfortunately the comment of his critics, even of those who admired him, tells a different story. "To say of this noble work that it is the best which ever appeared of the kind, would be speaking in much lower terms than it deserves," writes Melmoth, himself a successful translator, in *Fitzosborne's Letters*. Melmoth's description of Pope's method is, however, very different from that offered by Pope himself. "Mr. Pope," he says, "seems, in most places, to have been inspired with the same sublime spirit that animates his original; as he often takes fire from a single hint in his author, and blazes out even with a stronger and brighter flame of poetry. Thus the character of Thersites, as it stands in the English *Iliad*, is heightened, I think, with more masterly strokes of satire than appear in the Greek; as many of those similes in Homer, which would appear, perhaps, to a modern eye too naked and unornamented, are painted by Pope in all the beautiful drapery of the most graceful metaphor" — a statement backed by citation of the famous moonlight passage, which Melmoth finds finer than the corresponding passage in the original. There is no doubt in the critic's mind as to the desirability of improving upon Homer. "There is no ancient author," he declares, "more likely to betray an injudicious interpreter into meannesses than Homer… But a skilful artist knows how to embellish the most ordinary subject; and what would be low and spiritless from a less masterly pencil, becomes pleasing and graceful when worked up by Mr. Pope."[449]

Melmoth's last comment suggests Matthew Arnold's remark, "Pope composes with his eye on his style, into which he translates his object, whatever it may be,"[450] but in intention the two criticisms are very different. To the average eighteenth-century reader Homer was entirely acceptable "when worked up by Mr. Pope." Slashing Bentley might declare that it "must not be called Homer," but he admitted that "it was a pretty poem." Less competent critics, unhampered by Bentley's scholarly doubts, thought the work adequate both as a poem and as a translated poem. Dennis, in his *Remarks upon Pope's Homer*, quotes from a recent review some characteristic phrases. "I know not which I should most admire," says the reviewer, "the justness of the original, or the force and beauty of the language, or the sounding variety of the numbers."[451] Prior, with more honesty, refuses to bother his head over "the

---

[449]Pp. 53-4.

[450]*Essays*, Oxford Edition, p. 258.

[451]*Mr. Dennis's Remarks upon Pope's Homer*, London, 1717, p. 9.

justness of the original," and gratefully welcomes the English version.

> Hang Homer and Virgil; their meaning to seek,
> A man must have pok'd into Latin and Greek;
> Those who love their own tongue, we have reason to hope,
> Have read them translated by Dryden and Pope.[452]

In general, critics, whether men of letters or Grub Street reviewers, saw both Pope's *Iliad* and Homer's *Iliad* through the medium of eighteenth-century taste. Even Dennis's onslaught, which begins with a violent contradiction of the hackneyed tribute quoted above, leaves the impression that its vigor comes rather from personal animus than from distrust of existing literary standards or from any new and individual theory of translation.

With the romantic movement, however, comes criticism which presents to us Pope's *Iliad* as seen in the light of common day instead of through the flattering illusions which had previously veiled it. New translators like Macpherson and Cowper, though too courteous to direct their attack specifically against the great Augustan, make it evident that they have adopted new standards of faithfulness and that they no longer admire either the diction or the versification which made Pope supreme among his contemporaries. Macpherson gives it as his opinion that, although Homer has been repeatedly translated into most of the languages of modern Europe, "these versions were rather paraphrases than faithful translations, attempts to give the spirit of Homer, without the character and peculiarities of his poetry and diction," and that translators have failed especially in reproducing "the magnificent simplicity, if the epithet may be used, of the original, which can never be characteristically expressed in the antithetical quaintness of modern fine writing."[453] Cowper's prefaces show that

---

[452]In *Down Hall, a Ballad.*
[453]Preface to *The Iliad of Homer*, translated by James Macpherson, London, 1773.

he has given serious consideration to all the opinions of the theorists of his century, and that his own views are fundamentally opposed to those generally professed. His own basic principle is that of fidelity to his author, and, like every sensible critic, he sees that the translator must preserve a mean between the free and the close methods. This approval of compromise is not, however, a mere formula; Cowper attempts to throw light upon it from various angles. The couplet he immediately repudiates as an enemy to fidelity. "I will venture to assert that a just translation of any ancient poet in rhyme is impossible," he declares. "No human ingenuity can be equal to the task of closing every couplet with sounds homotonous, expressing at the same time the full sense of his original. The translator's ingenuity, indeed, in this case becomes itself a snare, and the readier he is at invention and expedient, the more likely he is to be betrayed into the wildest departures from the guide whom he professes to follow."[454] The popular idea that the translator should try to imagine to himself the style which his author would have used had he been writing in English is to Cowper "a direction which wants nothing but practicability to recommend it. For suppose six persons, equally qualified for the task, employed to translate the same Ancient into their own language, with this rule to guide them. In the event it would be found that each had fallen on a manner different from that of all the rest, and by probable inference it would follow that none had fallen on the right."[455]

Cowper's advocacy of Miltonic blank verse as a suitable vehicle for a translation of Homer need not concern us here, but another innovation on which he lays considerable stress in his prefaces helps to throw light on the practice and the standards of his immediate predecessors. With more veracity than Pope, he represents himself as having followed his author even in

---

[454]Preface to first edition, taken from *The Iliad of Homer, translated by the late William Cowper*, London, 1802.
[455]Preface to first edition, taken from *The Iliad of Homer, translated by the late William Cowper*, London, 1802.

his "plainer" passages. "The passages which will be least noticed, and possibly not at all, except by those who shall wish to find me at a fault," he writes in the preface to the first edition, "are those which have cost me abundantly the most labor. It is difficult to kill a sheep with dignity in a modern language, to slay and prepare it for the table, detailing every circumstance in the process. Difficult also, without sinking below the level of poetry, to harness mules to a wagon, particularizing every article of their furniture, straps, rings, staples, and even the tying of the knots that kept all together. Homer, who writes always to the eye with all his sublimity and grandeur, has the minuteness of a Flemish painter." In the preface to his second edition he recurs to this problem and makes a significant comment on Pope's method of solving it. "There is no end of passages in Homer," he repeats, "which must creep unless they be lifted; yet in all such, all embellishment is out of the question. The hero puts on his clothes, or refreshes himself with food and wine, or he yokes his steeds, takes a journey, and in the evening preparation is made for his repose. To give relief to subjects prosaic as these without seeming unseasonably tumid is extremely difficult. Mr. Pope abridges some of them, and others he omits; but neither of these liberties was compatible with the nature of my undertaking."[456]

That Cowper's reaction against Pope's ideals was not a thing of sudden growth is evident from a letter more outspoken than the prefaces. "Not much less than thirty years since," he writes in 1788, "Alston and I read Homer through together. The result was a discovery that there is hardly a thing in the world of which Pope is so entirely destitute as a taste for Homer... I remembered how we had been disgusted; how often we had sought the simplicity and majesty of Homer in his English representative, and had found instead of them puerile conceits, extravagant metaphors, and the tinsel of modern embellishment in every possible position."[457]

---

[456]*Preface prepared by Mr. Cowper for a Second Edition*, in edition of 1802.

Cowper's "discovery," startling, almost heretical at the time when it was made, is now little more than a commonplace. We have long recognized that Pope's Homer is not the real Homer; it is scarcely an exaggeration to say, as does Mr. Andrew Lang, "It is almost as if he had taken Homer's theme and written the poem himself."[458] Yet it is surprising to see how nearly the eighteenth-century ambition, "to write a poem that will live in the English language" has been answered in the case of Pope. Though the "tinsel" of his embellishment is no longer even "modern," his translation seems able to hold its own against later verse renderings based on sounder theories. The Augustan translator strove to give his work "elegance, energy, and fire," and despite the false elegance, we can still feel something of true energy and fire as we read the *Iliad* and the *Odyssey*.

The truth is that, in translated as in original literature the permanent and the transitory elements are often oddly mingled. The fate of Pope's Homer helps us to reconcile two opposed views regarding the future history of verse translations. Our whole study of the varying standards set for translators makes us feel the truth of Mr. Lang's conclusion: "There can be then, it appears, no final English translation of Homer. In each there must be, in addition to what is Greek and eternal, the element of what is modern, personal, and fleeting."[459] The translator, it is obvious, must speak in the dialect and move in the measures of his own day, thereby very often failing to attract the attention of a later day. Yet there must be some place in our scheme for the faith expressed by Matthew Arnold in his essays on translating Homer, that "the task of translating Homer into English verse both will be re-attempted, and may be re-attempted successfully."[460] For in translation there is involved

---

[457]*Letters*, ed. Wright, London, 1904, v. 3, p. 233.

[458]*s*, p. 384.

[459]Preface to *The Odyssey of Homer done into English Prose*.

[460]Lecture, III, in Essays, p. 311.

enough of creation to supply the incalculable element which cheats the theorist. Possibly some day the miracle may be wrought, and, in spite of changing literary fashions, we may have our English version of Homer in a form sufficient not only for an age but for all time.

It is this incalculable quality in creative work that has made theorizing on the methods of translation more than a mere academic exercise. Forced to adjust itself to the facts of actual production, theory has had to follow new paths as literature has followed new paths, and in the process it has acquired fresh vigor and flexibility. Even as we leave the period of Pope, we can see the dull inadequacy of a worn-out collection of rules giving way before the honest, individual approach of Cowper. "Many a fair precept in poetry," says Dryden apropos of Roscommon's rules for translation, "is like a seeming demonstration in the mathematics, very specious in the diagram, but failing in the mechanic operation."[461] Confronted by such discrepancies, the theorist has again and again had to modify his "specious" rules, with the result that the theory of translation, though a small, is yet a living and growing element in human thought.

---

[461]*Preface to Sylvae*, in *Essays*, v. 1, p. 252.

Vita

Born 1881, at Aurora, Ontario, Canada. Attended the Aurora Public School, the Aurora High School, the University of Toronto (1898-1902, B.A. 1902), the Ontario Normal College (1902-3), Columbia University (1908-9, 1910-12, A.M. 1909).

Made in United States
North Haven, CT
21 May 2022

19374072R10107